JOHN RENARD

Understanding the Islamic Experience

previously published as

In the Footsteps of Muhammad

PAULIST PRESS
New York/Mahwah, N.J.

Cover photo: Dome of the Sultan's Mosque (1980s) in Shah Alam, near Kuala Lumpur, Malaysia. This and all other photos in text are courtesy of the author. Cover design by Lynn Else.

Miscellaneous portions of the book's material appeared as parts of several articles previously published in *Studies in Formative Spirituality* 2:2 (May 1981), pp. 189–203, and 4:3 (November 1983), pp. 335–350, and in *Spirituality Today* 34:2 (Summer 1982), pp. 100–112, and 34:3 (Fall 1982), pp. 209–221. My thanks to the publishers of those two journals for permission to revise and rearrange some of that material. Unless otherwise noted, translations are the author's.

I wish to thank Geoff Grubb of Lourdes College for suggesting that Paulist Press might be interested in a book like this. For her help in preparing camera-ready tables, I thank Janice Harbaugh of St. Louis University.

ISBN: 0-8091-4096-9

Published by Paulist Press
997 Macarthur Boulevard
Mahwah, New Jersey 07430

www.paulistpress.com

Printed and bound in the United States of America

Contents

To my Parents
George and Virginia

Foreword

Three objectives have shaped this book. It seeks, first, to introduce a general audience to the global religio-cultural phenomenon known as Islam. Second, it responds at least indirectly to a number of urgent questions many American non-Muslims find themselves asking about Islam. Finally, it pursues the first two objectives by using metaphors drawn from within the Islamic tradition, in such a way that any Muslim readers would recognize the treatment as a reasonable and objective, but sympathetic, approach to their tradition.

In pursuit of the first objective, this essay differs from many introductions to Islam currently available. Instead of employing a topical organizing principle, in which such essentials as law, mysticism, scripture, prophet, and contemporary issues each has its own chapter, our approach emphasizes the experiential dimension. It begins with such questions as: How do Muslims see themselves and their tradition? How might their self-understanding and sense of Muslim identity impinge on non-Muslims? Several primary metaphors can help an outsider to appreciate the world view that is part of the heritage of Muslims.

Fulfilling the second presents a large challenge. We non-Muslims, especially those of us whose cultures are Euro-American, must be aware that we approach the phenomenon of Islam with a range of prejudices and stereotypes. Some of these are subtle; some, while not entirely obvious to us, are still rather blatant. Questions that recent and ongoing events in the Middle East naturally pose for us are important and valid. But we need to cultivate an awareness concerning the usually unchallenged assumptions that underlie those questions. In the demanding process of seeking such a sensitivity, we have to be ruthlessly honest in admitting that all of our questions arise from a particular point of view, and that ours is only one point of view among many. Any question we raise about "those people," whoever they may be, we have to be equally willing to put to ourselves. With that in mind, we can profitably round up and sort through some of those always fascinating and sometimes troubling issues that pop into many minds with the mere mention of Islam or the Middle East.

Our third objective, that of describing Islam in terms acceptable to Muslims, is similarly challenging. Obviously no outsider can portray an insider's truth in an altogether unbiased fashion. One can, nevertheless, listen carefully to the story of Islam as told by Islamic sources, and become attuned to the images and metaphors those sources use to communicate their core realities. The enterprise remains a bit presumptuous, but so long as we embark upon it with the willingness to continue revising our views, the venture promises a positive outcome. In any case, daily headlines and the rapid pace of change in our global home make such attempts at interreligious and intercultural understanding imperative.

When this volume first appeared, the United States and its coalition partners had become embroiled in "the Gulf War," ostensibly seeking to defend Kuwait and the Arabian peninsula as a whole against Iraqi aggression. Now, a decade later, the very presence of foreign troops in the land of Islam's birth figures prominently in the rationale articulated by extremist groups for the latest, and arguably the most devastating wave of terrorism ever unleashed. Led by Usama bin Laden's al-Qa'ida, extremists claiming Islamic religious justification for their actions call for the overthrow of the Saudi regime, whose legitimacy rests to a high degree on its guardianship of the "two sanctuaries" of Mecca and Medina. Saudi complicity in the foreign desecration of the sacred soil, American-led attacks on Iraq and Afghanistan, and the widespread perception among Muslims that the United States has done nothing to ease the plight of the Palestinian people top the list of explicit terrorist grievances.

This most recent metamorphosis of religiously-tinged rage presents a number of troubling aspects: seemingly random and indiscriminate violence, the black-and-white thinking that forecloses discussion and divides the world into believers and infidels, the determination to use *whatever* means their ends justify, and the apparent willingness of extremist warriors to commit suicide—to name but a few. But perhaps most distressing of all, from the perspective of religious and Islamic studies, is that the image of "Islam" these proponents of extreme measures present is tragically myopic. They would have us all believe that nearly fourteen hundred years of Islamic history since the death of Muhammad has been anything but Islamic. For them, that history is a gaping wound of godlessness, a vast cesspool of moral decay. Their worldview leaves no room for the rich array of Arab, Persian, Turkish, Indian, and scores of other major cultural legacies.

Their claims bristle with contradictions. They boast, on the one hand, that they are fighting for all 1.2 billion Muslims on earth, while on the other hand they condemn as un-Islamic the hundreds of millions who do not share their values. They demolish the great Buddhas of Bamiyan and lash out in puritanical righteousness at cultural icons of every kind. Yet they carefully manipulate global news media into creating of Usama bin Laden the most widely recognized image on the planet, his face plastered on countless posters, T-shirts and TV newscasts.

Extremist rejections of history and culture in the name of "pure" religious belief clarify nothing, however much they masquerade as a quest for the heart of the Islamic faith. The more they succumb to the false promise of absolute certitude, the more they try to seduce others into abandoning the honest quest for truth in the midst of often disconcerting ambiguity. This little volume, with a number of new features, reaffirms the conviction that one can arrive at a genuine understanding of such a complex and expansive reality as "Islam" only by setting it within the broadest possible contexts of history, culture, and symbolism.

Introduction

Sacred Footprints

Seek a greater understanding of the role of religious values in our world and in human history and one thing becomes increasingly evident: foundational figures have left their tracks everywhere. Traces of prophets and sages from Abraham to Zoroaster crisscross the landscapes of faith, marking off mountain and river, cave and open plain as sacred sites.

Sometimes those vestiges of holy presence have taken physical form. Believers of many traditions, paradoxically, revere images of the printless foot in stone or paint. Christian tradition discerns the footprints of Jesus on the Mount of Olives in Jerusalem as reminders of the Ascension. More than a few medieval pilgrims, including Ignatius of Loyola, set off for the Holy Land led by the desire to see those tangible remains of the Savior. Buddhist temples all over Asia maintain as their most prized relics images of the Buddha's perfect sole. Pilgrims to those sites have sometimes taken away as mementos of their journeys a drawing of the Enlightened One's print. Hindus have for centuries lavished fragrant petals of loving devotion on images of sacred feet, and have meditated on drawings of the feet of the deity Vishnu, whose outlines encompass the whole of sacred reality.

Muslims also have recognized in vestiges of printless feet both the presence of the holy and a form of guidance along the "straight path." In Makka (Mecca), the spiritual pivot of the universe, Muslims pay their respects to Abraham. According to one tradition, Abraham observed the construction of the Ka'ba standing on a stone, now enclosed in a copper and glass cupola and called the "station of Abraham." As confirmation of the veracity of his prophetic mission, God caused the stone beneath his feet to soften like wax. In that stone the eyes of belief see his mark. Muhammad, too, still walks the earth in spirit as he once did in the flesh. Whether in colorful stylized diagrams or solid three-dimensional imprints, the soles of Muhammad's feet and the sandals he wore have often provided a symbolic aniconic summary of the Prophet's meaning and legacy.

The most important sacred footprints remain not in stone or in manuscript illustrations, but etched on the hearts of believers. Journey metaphors abound in religious literature. Pilgrimage—easily the most obvious of those images—and the inward quest it symbolizes, is a virtually universal human phenomenon. An understanding of that and other forms of religious journeying can provide a significant vehicle for appreciating the meaning of all the major religious traditions. Pilgrimage practices, or even the loss thereof, offer clues as to how we humans have mapped out our cosmos. And since each religious tradition draws its own special map and prescribes its own unique set of provisions, images of the journey tell not only of how religious persons are alike the world over, but how they differ as well.

Muhammad as Exemplar

If one may speak of a moral and spiritual exemplar for the individual Muslim, a paradigm against which to assess one's own growth in faith and action, it is surely the Prophet Muhammad. Few personalities have gotten a more ample dose of vituperation and calumny over the centuries from the pens of Christian writers than Muhammad. Christians especially have seriously misunderstood the man and his meaning for scores of millions of Muslims. Vatican II does not mention Muhammad at all, perhaps out of a desire to avoid any semblance of controversy over Christian belief in the finality of Christ, as against the Muslim belief that God delivered the climactic revelation through Muhammad.

It is impossible to understand Islam without appreciating the place of the Prophet and members of his family as role-models. Jesus and the other pre-Islamic prophets hold similarly exemplary places in Islamic spirituality. As Vatican II acknowledges, Muslims do not consider Jesus divine but hold him in the profoundest reverence, along with his mother Mary. But Muhammad's role is final and definitive.

One of the things Muslims inevitably request of non-Muslim interpreters of their tradition is that we emphasize the well-deserved esteem in which they hold Muhammad. The Prophet's example is never far from the consciousness of the average Muslim. Beyond the myriad particular details of Muhammad's ordinary behavior that survive in the speech and actions of twentieth century Muslims, one can point to an overarching theme in his life that continues to provide Muslims with a larger spiritual structure and frame of reference. Muhammad was a wayfarer, a journeyer along what the Qur'an calls the Straight Path.

Two clusters of metaphors offer a way to understand the uniquely Islamic mode of religious sojourning. The first cluster surrounds the image of Muhammad as exemplary wayfarer and the need for Muslims to follow in his footsteps.

Three specific journeys in the Prophet's life stand out as especially significant and paradigmatic for Muslims. The first (not chronologically, but in terms of its foundational implications for the Muslim community) is that of the *Hijra* or Emigration from Makka to Madina in 622 C.E. That journey marks the official beginning of Muslim history, but in addition it has become a metaphor for a fundamental requirement of all Muslims in their relationship to the world around them. They must be willing to "leave home" symbolically; to hear God's call to establish a community of justice in an unjust world; to risk, as Abraham did long before Muhammad, the censure of a culture of unbelief in the interest of a community of faith and trust in God.

Muhammad's second symbolic journey was his Pilgrimage or *Hajj* to Makka from Madina toward the end of his life. From a religio-political perspective, it was a statement of control over the already ancient holy site. As for its symbolic spiritual implications, his pilgrimage was a return to a sacred center long before hallowed by the presence of Abraham. Ever since, Muslims have followed Muhammad's pilgrim steps, not only in a literal journey to Makka, but as lifelong sojourners and seekers after the divine center.

Finally, Muslims look to an early mystical experience in Muhammad's life. Tradition has it that God carried him by night from the "mosque of the sanctuary" in Makka to the "farther mosque" in Jerusalem, whence Muhammad ascended to the throne of God and was shown the various regions of the heavens and underworld. The first segment is called the Night Journey (*Isra'*), the second the Ascension (*Mi'raj*). Though no Muslim would presume to lay claim to Muhammad's exalted prerogatives, the Prophet's mystical journey has nevertheless remained an important paradigm of the spiritual life.

A second cluster of metaphors is closely related. Every traveler needs signs along the way and light by which to make them out for what they are. In several texts of the Qur'an, God speaks of showing "signs on the horizons" and "within their/your very selves." (Qur'an 41:53, 51:20–21) In addition the sacred text refers to itself as made up of "signs" or *ayat* (plural of *aya*), a word that has therefore come to mean "verses" as well. Hence the scripture is itself one large series of signs. Problem: Left to themselves, human beings are incapable of reading those signs adequately. Solution: The scripture explains in several lovely passages that God is himself the light of the heavens and the earth, that the fundamental mission of every prophet is to bring his people from darkness into light, and that the Qur'an stands as a light illuminating itself in its progressive unfolding.

Plan of the Book
(See Table 1, Schematic Overview Chart)

Four chapters, each divided into several sections, will integrate these two central and interrelated clusters of metaphors with some oft-asked questions about Islam. Each chapter begins by establishing a particular point of view from which it studies Islam. Chapter 1 views Islam as a faith tradition with historic precedent: Islam is not some new-fangled invention from the mind of Muhammad; it sees itself as part of a much larger history of divine call and human response. Chapter 2 then considers Islam as a religious tradition in relation to others: Muslims relate to a larger world, a world beyond the fringes of Islam, a world of religious persons with whom Muslims share a wide range of creation-centered concerns. The third chapter characterizes Islam as a unique community of faith, exclusive in membership and distinctive in its approach to life. Finally, Chapter 4 looks at ways in which Islam has provided for the spiritual needs of individual persons.

Chapter 1 deals with foundations of the Islamic tradition. The chapter seeks to respond to a number of questions

Table 1. In the Footsteps of Muhammad: A Schematic Overview of the Book

Chapter/Point of View — Islam seen as:	Prophetic Paradigm	Revelation		Response			
		Signs/Theaters of Revelation	Light/Guidance Divine Imagery	Experienced In	Expressed In	Context of Journey	Goal of Journey
Tradition with Historic Precedent (Ch. I)	Abraham/Khalil Moses/Kalim	Life of Muhammad	Creator, Judge Mercy, Compassion	Muhammad/ Prophet/ Wayfarer	Arabic Qur'an Hadith	Hijra/Hajj Isra-Mi'raj	Toward God, bring people from darkness to light
Global in relation to non-Islamic world (Ch. II)	Hijra	"Horizons" = Whole of Creation	God as Light of Heaven and Earth	Humankind / Natural World	Ritual/Myth / Natural Symbols	"Terrain" of all Creation	Right Relation to Cosmos
Unique Community of Faith (Ch. III)	Hajj	Scriptural Verse = Aya = Sign	Qur'an as Light Illuminating Itself	Islamic Institutions: Scripture (Authority), Prophet (Succession), History	Creedal Language Across Range of Tradition: Imams, Law Schools Sunni, Shi'i ⟨12-er / 7-er⟩	Straight Path Main Road, Shari'a	Build and Foster All-Inclusive Global Community
Individual Spiritual Wisdom (Ch. IV)	Isra & Mi'raj	The Self, Each Person	Light God Casts into the Heart	Personal Relationship to God	Language of Mysticism/ Personal Prayer	Each Person's Path Tariqa	Authentic Self-Knowledge, Intimate Awareness of God

non-Muslims frequently ask: Do Muslims worship some "other" God? And is this "Allah" really as stern and demanding—even warlike—as some seem to think? What do Muslims think of God? Would I as a non-Muslim have anything in common with Muslims in this regard? And what about their holy book? Didn't Muhammad just end up borrowing from the Bible? Why are some of its stories like, but still different from, biblical materials? How could a religious leader be a spiritual example if he was so involved in mundane affairs, and even military matters, as Muhammad was?

Of Chapter 1's three sections, the first focuses on God as creator, light and guide, as the one who lays out the terrain on which all humanity journeys, and then offers guidance. The second discusses the Qur'an and Muslims' understanding of it as a source of light and guidance to them as a distinct and exclusive community of faith. Finally, Muhammad's role as example for wayfarers looks at crucial events in his life and at why he remains such a pivotal figure for Muslims. Each section places its topic within the broader context of Islam's relationships with other religious traditions, specifically, Judaism and Christianity.

Chapter 2 then moves to the first of the paradigmatic journeys in the life of Muhammad. It describes how his Hijra has become a model of "striving in the way of God" and a metaphor of how each Muslim is called to leave home by placing all trust in God. Since Muhammad's journey took him away from the known to the unknown, Muslims have extended its metaphorical meaning to include the whole range of issues surrounding Islam in relation to the world outside itself. Some questions the chapter seeks to address are these: Is Islam inherently an expansionist, missionary movement? If so, do Muslims intend to take over the world, converting everyone to their way of thinking? What of all the talk one hears about declaring "jihad" against the infidels? Does

Islam condone and even promote war and such things as the taking of hostages and terrorism? Why do so many Muslims, especially in the Middle East, seem to react so violently to the presence of outsiders? Don't they appreciate help in advancing beyond traditional ways that seem so backward? Do Muslims have a concern for social and economic justice anything like that of, say, Christianity and Judaism? Do Muslims want to "dialogue" with non-Muslims?

Chapter 2's first section will treat the concept of Hijra as metaphor. After looking at how the Muslim community responds to "signs on the horizons," expressing its right relationship to all creation, we turn to the notion of Islam as part of the larger community of humanity, its sense of relationships to the non-Muslim world. The third section will discuss such issues as peace and war, justice, environmental concerns, the search for an Islamic economics, and Islam's encounter with other religious traditions, especially to the Peoples of the Book. Here issues such as religious liberty under Islam, tolerance, the prospects for interreligious dialogue, and Islam's notion of "vying with one another in good deeds" will arise.

Chapter 3 brings together the notion of God's revelation (i.e. signs and light) to the Muslim community as a unique community of faith, with Muhammad's second paradigmatic journey. By means of his pilgrimage (Hajj), Muhammad symbolized the journey of Muslims together back to their spiritual center along the "Main Road" of the divinely revealed law (*Shari'a*). This chapter has in mind such questions as: How did Makka become so central in Islam's geography? Why do Muslims feel so protective about their holy places, so averse to having foreign troops—for example—anywhere near them? Why do Muslims seem to hold on to what Americans think are outmoded social practices, especially with respect to women's social and cultural roles? What sense can one make of the welter of conflicting claims and factions that seem to operate within the Islamic world—especially the Middle East?

The chapter begins with a look at Hajj as metaphor for the Muslim community's journey together back to the center. A section on "Signs Among Believers" discusses ways in which Muslims have looked upon themselves as a unique community of faith. Models of leadership, including the implications of the Sunni/Shi'i division and related historical issues, and the development of institutions of authority form the topics of the next two sections. Finally, the chapter sums up a wide range of ways in which Muslims have given expression to their belief and membership in the community of Islam.

Chapter 4 takes its cue from Muhammad's third paradigmatic journey, his "Night Journey and Ascension," as metaphor for the individual spiritual path. As the Qur'an indicates, God chooses to show people signs "within their very selves" so that they might understand. In the background are such not infrequently asked questions as: Do Muslims have a sense of a personal relationship to God? Isn't the main emphasis on the collectivity and on the individual's being too lowly to presume a direct relationship to the creator? What about the Muslim's sense of personal direction in life, of personal purpose? Does Islam stress heavily the idea of absolute predestination? What of individual responsibility and moral freedom? Does Islam have any sort of mystical tradition or notion of saintliness or personal holiness like that of Christianity? Do Muslims have a sense of deep spiritual values, or is religion more a question of fulfilling external obligations?

The first section leads off with the metaphorical significance of Isra' and Mi'raj and continues by looking at the nature of the "signs within the self." The individual's personal spiritual trajectory is the journey toward meeting with the Creator. After an outline of the key themes in the history of Islamic spirituality and mystical tradition, we discuss matters of Islamic spiritual direction and personal prayer. Finally the chapter looks at how the Islamic tradition deals with the mysteries of death and the end of the earthly journey.

By way of conclusion, the Epilogue describes the coming of Islam to the Americas as the last leg of its global journey. Non-Muslim Americans can no longer think of Islam either as an alien creed espoused by exotic peoples in faraway lands, or as a small religious splinter faction within American society. Islam has become as much an "American" religious tradition as Judaism and Christianity. And the journey continues.

1

Mapping the Straight Path: The Foundations of Islamic Religious Experience

Islam as a religious tradition developed in the rich religious and cultural matrix of the Middle East. With its three foundational theological elements, Islam stands firm in the line of the Abrahamic monotheistic faiths. Belief in an omnipotent creative deity, in the centrality of a revealed sacred scripture, and in the necessity of prophets to communicate the mind of the deity to humankind links Islam explicitly to Judaism and Christianity. The present chapter discusses some implications of the connections among the three traditions, viewing Islam in terms of its historic precedents. In keeping with the organizing theme of journey, we shall focus especially on how images of God as creator and guide, of the Qur'an as light and guidance, and of Muhammad as wayfarer inform an Islamic approach to life.

Non-Muslims are often surprised, even shocked, to hear that Islam's central spiritual and ethical presuppositions are virtually identical to those of Judaism and Christianity. Why then, many people ask, do Jews, Christians, and Muslims not get along better, especially in the Middle East? Perhaps the best response to that and similar queries is that strife is simply endemic to the human race. Why do the Catholics and Protestants of Northern Ireland hold so tenaciously to their ancient rivalries and hatred? They are, of course, all Christians. Most Christians and Jews will find it simple enough to distin-

Mihrab and *minbar* (pulpit) of Mamluk Sultan Hasan
madrasa complex (1356–63), Cairo.

guish between what individuals or groups do and the ideals and values for which a faith tradition stands—at least when it comes to their own. However, non-Muslims too often and too readily equate the behavior of a minority of Muslims, generally identified as extremist, fundamentalist, revolutionary, right-wing fanatics, with the whole of a tradition and the generality of its adherents.

A sad fact of human history has been that communities of persons—ethnic, political, economic, or religious—tend to become closed systems bent on defending themselves against the threat posed by other such communities. That their religious affiliations are more often blamed for factionalism and intolerance than other equally liable forces is really only a testimony to the intensity of the emotional responses religious language and imagery can elicit.

What if one could approach the study of Islam (or any religious or cultural tradition, for that matter) free of the prejudices and suspicions that so easily cloud one's vision and skew one's judgment of other persons? Though none of us can claim true objectivity, we can at least begin with the assumption that the qualities we have the greatest difficulty accepting in another reflect in large measure what we cannot accept in ourselves.

Much of the allegedly objective journalism that has fed American curiosity about the Middle East in recent years fairly reeks of condescension and thinly veiled bigotry. One television correspondent, reporting on the aftermath of the Persian Gulf conflict, characterized Saudi Arabia's policy as "Pray and pay: pray to Allah, and pay anyone who can provide" necessary services and protection. The tone of his remark was inherently demeaning, but, beyond that, it seemed to suggest that Christian America and Jewish Israel would of course never rely on such a strategy. In any case, though Allah may hear Saudi prayers, God has his ear turned elsewhere.

One could cite numerous examples of that peculiar attitude. Just after the cease-fire in the Persian Gulf hostilities, another reporter interviewed a young soldier who had secured as souvenirs an AK-47 rifle and a Qur'an. Asked what he intended to do with the book, the soldier replied that he would spend some time reading about what sort of being "this Allah" was. He clearly expected the worst, but he did not find it strange to be fighting shoulder to shoulder with troops who read the same scripture as the enemy.

Islamic Images of God

But who is "this Allah" of whom Muslims speak? Many non-Muslims have the impression that the term Allah refers to some despotic deity with a taste for violence and infidel blood. Perhaps that is because so many television and movie images of Muslim soldiers depicts them screaming "Allahu Akbar" (God is supreme) as they attack or celebrate victory. How is it, many wonder, that they seem so ready to associate Allah with violence? In Arabic, the word Allah is simply a compound of *al-* (the definite article, "the") and *ilah* (god, deity). Joined together, they signify "God." Nearly all Arabic speakers, including Iraqi Jews and Syrian Christians, refer to their Supreme Being as Allah.

Images of God are central to virtually every religious tradition, and crucial to one's understanding of how religious motivation works. For now we shall focus on some Islamic images, postponing until Chapter 2 a specific look at the matter of *jihad* (justifiable struggle, religiously sanctioned warfare) and other forms of ostensibly religious violence non-Muslims often associate with the "God of Islam."

Most of us tend to believe that God is on our side—even those who do not believe in God except when it suits their purposes. Proprietary ideas of who God is, what God likes and dislikes, and how God deals with human problems make it very challenging indeed to open one's mind to the images of God that other people hold dear. Never mind that if God is as big as most religious traditions claim, God has the option of being on everyone's side. That little piece of logic soon gets swept under the rug, for it works havoc with the human penchant for sanctifying divisions and enmities with claims to divine favor.

Images of God prevalent in one religious tradition inevitably overlap with those of another, but each tradition has its distinctive tone and emphasis. Christians, for example, who find it quaint and dangerous that Muslims believe God has prepared rewards in paradise for those who die a martyr's death, might well recall that Christianity too has its tradition of martyrdom. If Jews and Christians take offense at the idea that the God of Islam sanctions certain forms of violence, they would do well to recall not only the just war theory, but the shockingly sanguinary images of God in Deuteronomy and other early sections of the Hebrew scriptures. Religious persons understandably gravitate to those images of God, already embedded in their traditions, that help explain the circumstances in which they find themselves. Similarly, if asked to reflect on the matter, most of us would likely assume that our most cherished (or dreaded) images of God are very close to those of the person next to us on the synagogue bench or the church pew. We might be surprised to discover that in fact our images of God bear a greater likeness to those of the Muslim in the mosque across town than to those of our co-religionist.

Most Jews and Christians are convinced their God is loving and kind, provident and generous, as well as thirsty for justice and equity. So are most Muslims. Of the "Ninety-Nine Most Beautiful Names" of God, the two by far most frequent-

ly invoked are "Gracious or Compassionate" and "Merciful."
All but one of the Qur'an's 114 *suras* (chapters) begins with
the phrase, "In the name of God, the Gracious and Merciful."
One might say these two names are as important for Muslims
as are the names Father, Son, and Holy Spirit heard in so
many Christian invocations. Virtually every Muslim public
speaker begins with that Qur'anic phrase, and goes on to wish
the audience the blessings and mercy of God.

The opening chapter of the Qur'an sets the tone of
prayer for Muslims, and lays the foundation for our present
consideration:

> In the Name of God, the Compassionate and Merciful:
>   Praise to God, Lord of the Universe.
> The Compassionate, the Merciful,
> Master of the Day of Judgment.
> You alone do we serve; from you alone do we seek help.
> Lead us along the Straight Path,
> the path of those who experience the shower of your grace,
> not of those who have merited your anger
> or of those who have gone astray. (Qur'an 1:1-7)

Here one finds clues to several of the principal divine attributes. Compassion and mercy top the list and receive an
emphatic second mention. In addition, God rules the "two
worlds" (seen and unseen, i.e. the universe), takes account at
Judgment, offers aid and grace, and manifests a wrathful side
to those who prefer arrogant independence from the origin of
all things. At the center of the prayer, the Muslim asks for
guidance on the Straight Path, a path laid out and marked as
the way of divine graciousness.

Not one of the Ninety-Nine Names of God, on which
Muslims meditate as they finger the thirty-three beads of the

rosary, will sound a dissonant note in the ear of Christian or Jew. All of those names conjure up images of God. Islamic tradition has divided the names into those that express an awareness of God's beauty and approachability (*jamal*), and those that evoke a sense of the divine majesty and awe-inspiring power (*jalal*). These references to the two sides of God recall the theological distinction between immanence and transcendence. God is both near and accessible—closer even than the jugular vein, according to Qur'an 50:16—and infinitely beyond human experience and imagining. Rudolf Otto's classic definition of the "holy" can further clarify the matter. The great German thinker calls the "sacred" or "holy" "the mystery both terrifying and fascinating." "Mystery" refers to irreducible, unanalyzable meaning, before which one can only stand silent. Still, paradoxically, one who experiences mystery cannot but be filled simultaneously with intimations of both irresistible attractiveness and sheer dread.[1] One thinks, for example, of Moses' curiosity at the sight of the burning bush and of his terror at finding himself in the presence of the Living God. He is riveted between the desire to flee and wanting to stay forever. The Qur'anic rendition of the story darkens the already dramatic scene with a nighttime setting.

Though all religious traditions ultimately strive to give expression to the total experience of divine mystery, each has its distinctive ways of emphasizing one or other aspect. Whereas Christianity's central doctrine of Incarnation tips the scale toward divine immanence, Islamic imagery tends to interpret the experience of God rather in terms of transcendence and majesty. This is only a very rough and relative characterization, however; Christians also view God as beyond human grasp, and as we shall see later, Islamic tradition has also known God as an intimate companion. It is fair to say that most images of God both enjoy seasons of prominence and suffer periods of relative disuse in the history of every religious tradition. On balance, however, the Islamic tradition has generally preferred images of divine majesty.

One fascinating image that is both highly instructive and easily misinterpreted is that of the divine ruse. One occasionally hears non-Muslims characterize Islam's God as wily or tricky, as though God delighted in cruel hoaxes. Not so. The Qur'an refers to God as "best of those who devise schemes" (see e.g. Qur'an 3:47, 8:30, 13:42, 27:51) to indicate that no human being can know the mind of God. Al-Ghazali, one of Islam's greatest pastoral theologians, develops the idea further. Partially because of its shock value, Ghazali sees in the divine stratagem (*makr*) the ultimate reminder that human beings are better off not trying to second-guess their creator. Ghazali tells the story of how once when Gabriel was with Muhammad, the two acknowledged to each other that they felt stark terror in the presence of God. God then spoke to them to reassure them; they need not be afraid, for He had made them secure. Should they indeed be unafraid? Muhammad wondered; had not God Himself told them not to tremble? Gabriel cautioned that they should not banish their fear too casually, regardless of the apparent meaning of God's words; they were, after all, in the presence of *God*. There only a fool would know no dread.[2] This arresting image is meant to emphasize God's utter transcendence of human imagining. A human being who thinks he or she has God down to a pattern has wandered from the Straight Path into the realm of presumptiousness. Let no one imagine that God is so boring as to be predictable.

Numerous verses of the Qur'an emphasize God's sovereignty and power. Two such texts come to mind. The first, called the "Throne Verse," appears as an inscription around

the interior of domes in dozens of major mosques across
the world:

> God—there is no deity but He; the Living, the Everlast-
> ing. Neither slumber nor sleep overcomes Him. To Him
> belong all that heavens and earth encompass. Who can
> intercede with Him, except by his leave? He knows all
> that surrounds [created beings], while they can grasp
> nothing of what He knows, except as He chooses. His
> Throne stretches across heaven and earth; sovereignty
> over them tires Him not, for He is the Exalted, the Mag-
> nificent. (Qur'an 2:255)

God is thus the beginning and end of all things, the Creator,
the Sustainer, the Provider, the Lord of space and time. According to a saying of Muhammad, the Throne Verse, like all
the Qur'an, has existed eternally in the mind of God and was
known to earlier prophets:

> Anas ibn Malik related that the Prophet said, "God re-
> vealed to Moses, 'Whoever continues to recite the Throne
> Verse after every prayer, on him will I bestow more than
> that granted to those who are ever thankful. His reward
> shall be as great as that of prophets and that granted the
> righteous for their good deeds. I shall spread over him
> my right hand in mercy. Nothing would hinder him from
> entering Paradise' . . . Moses said, 'My Lord, how can
> anyone hear this and not continue to observe it?' God
> said, 'I grant this to no one except a prophet, a righteous
> person, a man I love . . .' "[3]

Later in the chapter we shall return to the text briefly to discuss some issues related to the interpretation of scripture.

One of the great writers who have elaborated on the
theme of God's transcendence is the Persian Sana'i of Ghazna

(d. 1131, in what is now Afghanistan). He writes in the preface to his mystical didactic epic, the *Garden of Ultimate Reality:*

> O you who nourish the soul and ornament the visible world,
> And you who grant wisdom and are indulgent with those
>   who lack it;
> Creator and sustainer of space and of time,
> Custodian and provider of dweller and dwelling;
> All is of your making, dwelling and dweller,
> All is within your compass, time and space.
> Fire and air, water and earth,
> All are mysteriously within the scope of your power.
> All that is between your Throne and this earth
> Are but a fraction of your handiwork;
> Inspirited intelligence acts as your swift herald,
> Every living tongue that moves in every mouth
> Has but one purpose: to give you praise.
> Your sublime and exalted names
> Evidence your beneficence and grace and kindness.
> Every one of them outstrips throne and globe and dominion;
> They are a thousand plus one and a hundred less one.
> But to those who are outside the spiritual sanctuary,
> The names are veiled.
> O Lord, in your largesse and mercy
> Allow this heart and soul a glimpse of your name![4]

A second Qur'anic text, perhaps even more important as an architectural inscription than the "Throne Verse," offers a magnificently imaginative glimpse of the unimaginable. The "Verse of Light" provides another ingredient in our complex of imagery.

> God is the Light of Heaven and Earth. Picture His light as
> a niche within which there is a lamp, and the lamp is
> within a glass. And it is as though the glass were a glitter-
> ing star lit from a sacred olive tree neither of east nor

west, whose oil would fairly radiate even without the touch of fire. Light upon light, and God guides to His light whom He will. (Qur'an 24:35)

That text has inspired marvelous designs on prayer carpets and on the niches (*mihrab,* indicates orientation toward Makka) of mosques all over the world. It suggests several relevant issues in this context. First, it recalls the symbolism of the revelatory cosmic tree, one that glows without being consumed and is so large it spans the universe (neither of east nor of west). On the level of imagery, the text has functioned as a kind of summary, like the Throne Verse, of divine qualities.

Second, the last line brings to mind a question that has been significant in shaping Islamic intellectual history, namely, the matter of divine ordination of events or predestination. If God guides whom He will, then does He also *not* will to guide others? And if so, could those others truly be held responsible if they lose their way? The issue is complex. Suffice it to say for the moment that Islamic tradition has generally striven to strike a balance between God's unlimited power and the human person's limited freedom and commensurate accountability. It is useful to think of the apparent predilection for some form of divine predetermination as an analogy to the biblical phenomenon of God's "hardening the heart" of Pharaoh and even some of the people of Israel. We will return to this issue in Chapter 4 as we consider what Islamic tradition has to say to the individual believer.

Finally, the Verse of Light alludes to that crucial divine function of guidance, and that in turn brings us back to the image of journey. "Guide" is one of the ninety-nine names, and the Qur'an often speaks of God in that capacity. Just after the Throne Verse, the scripture continues: "God is the Guardian of those who believe; He brings them forth from darkness into His light. Those who arrogantly choose not to

Central dome and flanking half-domes, showing the
"Turkish pendentive" triangles that form the zone of
transition from square to circle, Ottoman Turkish,
Sulaymaniye Mosque (1550–57) in Istanbul. Qur'anic
verses adorn the circular and semicircular medallions.

believe will be led from the light into darkness, there to become companions of the fire forever." (Qur'an 2:257) The irony, in view of the Verse of Light, is striking. Those who rely on themselves cannot discover the authentic light, but come only to that fire that is darkness itself.

According to some interpreters God's relationship to journeying goes beyond the function of guidance. A widely influential and prolific thinker named Ibn Arabi (born in Spain, d. 1240) elaborates on the connections. He discerns sixteen journeys in the Qur'an. God begins by taking the primordial journey from the utter transcendence and inaccessibility of Sublimity downward to His Throne. From there God dispatches Creation on its journey from non-being into being and sends down the Qur'an. Adam He sends on the Journey of Calamity from paradise to earth. Noah embarks on the Journey of Safety and Moses on the Journey of Divine Appointment to meet God (we will shortly recall how Moses' chief attribute is that he conversed with God).

In Ibn Arabi's view, and that of other important mystics before and since, every spiritual journey is one of three types. There are journeys away from, toward, and in God. The first occurs when God banishes a fallen angel, when shame drives a sinner away, or when God sends a prophet or messenger into the world. Second, though all beings travel toward God, not all reach their goal. Unrepentant sinners experience the frustration of endless wandering; those who have obeyed but remain imperfect in their acknowledgment of the absolute unity and sovereignty of God arrive in the divine presence but are veiled from the divine vision; the elect find the ultimate goal. Of those who journey in God, some (known as philosophers) falter along the way because they rely on the rational faculty; the elect, saints, and prophets make easy progress.[5]

As we shall see shortly, the essential mediatorial role of prophets is to lead people from darkness to light. Speaking of the mission of Moses and his brother Aaron, Qur'an 37:117–8 says: "We [God speaking] gave them the Book that clarifies, and led them to the Straight Path." We turn now to consider, first, Islam's scripture within the context of the larger history of revelation, and, second, the place of Muhammad within the history of prophethood.

The Qur'an and the History of Revelation

> It is He [God] who sent down [revealed] to you the Book, confirming in truth all that preceded it; and before that He had sent down the Torah and the Gospel as guidance to humankind . . . (Qur'an 3:3)

Among the many foundations of Islamic religious tradition that intrigue and often puzzle non-Muslims, the Qur'an surely ranks high. First-time readers with some knowledge of biblical narratives are invariably struck by the frequent allusions to familiar tales of Adam and Eve, Abraham, Moses, David and Solomon, Jesus and Mary. Christians, especially, marvel that an entire chapter (Sura 19) is named after Mary, and that Jesus' mother is actually mentioned more often by name in the Qur'an than in the Greek Testament (the Christian scripture).

More careful examination of the scriptures, such as a comparison of the story of Joseph in Sura 12 with the account in Genesis 37 to 50, inevitably raises numerous questions for Muslims and non-Muslims alike. When Christians and Jews discover a Qur'anic Moses or Joseph, or Jesus or Mary, who do and say things evidently at variance with the biblical narratives, they often conclude that the Qur'an must be a slightly modified "borrowing." Muslims, on the other hand, explain discrepancies as evidence that Jews and Christians have obviously tampered with the original revelation to make it more palatable and less demanding. If fact, some argue, had the earlier "Peoples of the Book" not altered the record, God would not have needed to restore the revelation to its pristine purity by sending Muhammad with a corrective message. Besides, Muslim tradition adds, Muhammad was illiterate and therefore could not have plagiarized biblical material.

Neither point of view is very helpful, for both conclusions arise rather out of a spirit of partisan competition than out of a desire to deal openly with the data of history. The arguments seek only to defend the integrity of one scripture at the expense of the other. True, a great deal is at stake here, but only to the degree that we are unable to take the larger view of God's communication with humankind.

One possibility Christians and Jews might profitably explore is this. Just as stories of the great religious figures do not belong exclusively to any people or culture, so their capacity to reveal divine truth belongs to all whom God wishes to have access to them. Stories are a free-floating possession of humanity. If variations on narratives some associate with the Bible occur in the Qur'an, they are there for an important purpose that transcends the rights of Christians and Jews to claim exclusive ownership of "their" stories and truths.

Muslims, for their part, might well understand the Qur'an as bringing a new perspective, reinforcing the ancient message, and enhancing and multiplying the opportunities for human beings to respond in faith. More than one Muslim author has suggested that Muhammad's "illiteracy" functions in Islamic theology much the way Mary's virginity functions in Christianity. In neither case does the human being strive to initiate. In both instances, it is God who effects the wonder of sending His word into the world. For Christians, Mary is the medium for the Word made Flesh; for Muslims, Muhammad serves as the instrument by which the Word is made Book.[6] The "Inlibration" thus parallels the "Incarnation."

The Qur'an itself suggests an explanation for the very controversy at hand here:

> Humankind were once a single community. God sent prophets with news and warnings, and through them revealed the Book in truth that He might judge between people when they disagreed with one another. But, after the clear indicators had come to them, it was only out of self-centered stubbornness that they differed among themselves. God guided those who believed to the truth over which they argued, for God guides to the Straight Path whom He will. (Qur'an 2:213)

Before considering further such important issues as the place of the Qur'an in Islamic life and various modes of interpretation, it will be helpful to sum up briefly some of the Qur'an's most important formal qualities and themes.

As an historic event the revelation of the Arabic Qur'an defined a community of faith as its fundamental source of authority. Unlike either the Hebrew or Greek Testaments, the Qur'an unfolded over a relatively short period of time and its articulation is attributed to only one human being. Beginning in about 610 C.E., when he was about forty years old, Muhammad began to experience, in mostly auditory but occasionally visual form, what he would come to identify as divine revelations delivered by the angel Gabriel. Muhammad initially delivered the message orally, somewhat in the form of homiletical material. Not until more than two decades after the Prophet's death would a more or less definitive text be compiled and written. Tradition has divided the text into two main periods, the Makkan and Madinan, corresponding to the years before and after the Hijra, the move to

Madina in 622 C.E. Scholars have more recently further divided the Makkan period into very early, early, middle, and late periods, on the basis of the form and content of the suras.

Five themes appear most often in the earliest suras. Evidently presuming belief in some deity on the part of their hearers, they emphasize God's creative power, providence, and guidance. There was at first no emphasis on belief in only one God. Second, they speak of accountability at judgment in a rather general way, without specific reference to particular reward or punishment as motivation for upright behavior. In view of these two, the suras suggest that the appropriate response for the individual is a combination of gratitude and worship. The former flows out of an inner recognition of one's total dependence on God expressed formally in prayer. Parallel social consequences are acknowledged in the need for generosity as expressed in giving to those in need and seeking a just distribution of wealth. Finally the early message includes the theme of Muhammad's dawning awareness of his own prophetic mission and all that it would demand of him.

During the middle Makkan period, both the tone and the content of the suras began to change. Stories first of indigenous Arabian and then of biblical prophets illustrated graphically the disastrous consequences attendant upon refusal to hear the prophetic message. Here one finds a growing insistence on monotheistic belief and forthright condemnation of idolatry. Toward the end of the Makkan period, emphasis on the rejection of past prophets grew apace with Muhammad's own experience of local opposition. During the Madinan period, 622–632 C.E., both the style and the content changed dramatically. Whereas the Makkan suras tended to be poetic in tone, a form called rhymed prose (*saj'*), and quite dramatic, the later message became more prose-like. Its content reflected the growing need to regulate the daily life of the expanding community of Muslims, and the reality of increased contact with Christians and Jews (of whom several large tribes played a major part in the life of Madina).[7]

Over a period of twenty-three years or so, the divine interventions would come upon Muhammad in a variety of circumstances, often at times when he was struggling with a particular problem or issue. For example, for a while after the Hijra, the Muslims faced Jerusalem when they prayed, as did the local Jews. Apparently some friction caused a falling out with the Jewish community, causing Muhammad concern over the continued symbolic statement of the prayer orientation. Came the revelation, "We have seen you turning your face about toward the heavens. We shall now turn you toward a direction (*qibla*) that you will find satisfying. Turn your face toward the Mosque of the Sanctuary (site of the Ka'ba in Makka); wherever you are, turn your faces toward it." (Qur'an 2:144) That verse sometimes serves as a decorative inscription over the *mihrab* (niche) in mosques.

The Qur'an forms the core of all Islamic worship and devotional activity. As part of the daily ritual prayer, Muslims regularly recite the opening sura quoted earlier, as well as several other short pieces. An example is the very brief Sura 112 *al-Ikhlas* (Sincerity or Purity of Faith): "Proclaim: He is One God, God the besought of all; He does not beget; He is not begotten; and there is none like Him." It is unmistakably a reminder to Muslims that they are different from Christians with their belief in Father, Son, and Spirit. But perhaps just as important as the theological content is the sheer physical experience of reciting and/or hearing recitation of the Qur'an. The effect on listeners is often profound, for the mode of delivery combined with the extraordinarily earthy sound of Arabic makes for an intensely moving experience. One commentator has likened the recitation to the Christian practice of Communion, in that in both instances one has the Word on the tongue.[8]

Qur'an recitation is also part of many religious occasions outside the five daily prayers. After a funeral, families of the deceased often hire a reciter to come and grace the time for condolence with appropriate scriptural texts. During the fasting month of Ramadan, Muslims make a special place for recitation. They commemorate the 27th of that lunar month as the "Night of Power," when Muhammad received the first revelation. In addition, the entire Qur'an is recited during the thirty nights of Ramadan. For that and other such "liturgical" purposes, the text of the scripture has been divided into thirty sections, each of which is further halved, and those halves further quartered, yielding a total of 240 divisions. One can easily keep track of how far one has to go during each period of recitation.

There are further social dimensions as well. All across the Islamic world, the art of Qur'an recitation is highly prized. One can almost always tune in to a radio station that broadcasts recitation and commentary all day. In some places, such as Malaysia and Indonesia and even on a smaller scale here in the United States, the art has become very competitive. National contests draw huge crowds to sports stadiums, and winners look forward to going to a grand final meet in Makka. And in virtually any large Cairene mosque, for example, one can find people sitting alone and chanting their recitation quietly to themselves, or engaged in lively discussions about the text.

On the level of individual devotion as well, the Qur'an functions prominently. Some Muslims still strive to memorize the entire book, whose approximately 6,000 verses make it roughly the length of the New Testament. Memorizing the text means having it in one's heart and "keeping" it there. Paralleling the memorization of the Qur'an is what has been called the Qur'anization of the memory. The phrase originally referred to the intensely scriptural way of thinking mani-

fested by some of the great Muslim spiritual writers and
mystical poets. But there are further implications as well.
Especially throughout the Arabic speaking world, phrases
from the Qur'an have become an integral part of ordinary
speech.

Islamic tradition has known several important varieties
of scriptural interpretation or exegesis. In the last section we
looked at two of the Qur'an's premier texts, the Throne Verse
and the Verse of Light. We shall return to them shortly for
some insight into how Muslims have interpreted their scripture. The Qur'an itself makes a foundational observation as to
the two principal ways human beings might understand its
verses. "He it is who has revealed the Book to you. Some of its
verses/signs are categorical in meaning. They are the mother
(i.e. essence) of the Book. Others are open to interpretation
(i.e. metaphorical or allegorical). Those whose hearts harbor
ill-will pursue its metaphorical verses, in their desire for dis-
harmony and esoteric interpretation (*ta'wil*). None but God
knows the inner meaning." (Qur'an 3:7) That short text is
remarkable in its succinct articulation of the central difficulty
all scripture-based traditions must face. The text clearly
comes down on the side of clarity and literal meaning. Unfortunately, it leaves unanswered the question why it contains
the unambiguous at all.

We shall call the first type of interpretation the legal or
juristic. For all Muslims, Qur'an is at the very heart of all
religious law, followed in short order by sayings attributed to
Muhammad, called *Hadith*. It is the task of the legal scholar to
search the text for the clearest, least ambiguous references to
a given regulatory matter (from dietary law to family inheritance to criminal sanctions). What the jurist wants is to interpret the scripture so as to extend its applicability to present
needs and circumstances, even if those were not obviously
foremost at the time of the revelation.

A second type of exegesis is the theological. Ever since at least the late seventh or early eighth century, Muslims have been asking difficult questions about how the sacred text communicates the divine mystery. The imagery of God seated on the Throne has been at the center of much discussion in classical Islamic theology, for it raises the question of whether and to what degree one ought to interpret scripture literally. Taken literally, the text conjures up anthropomorphic pictures of the deity: there is a Throne and God actually sits upon it, and so forth. Taken metaphorically, the text becomes a colorful reference to divine sovereignty and transcendence. Islamic tradition has on the whole considered the latter option a dangerous invitation to water down the meaning of the sacred text.

Two of the principal positions in the theological debate are those of a group called the Mu'tazilites and the school of a man named al-Ash'ari (d. 944). A fundamental tenet of the Mu'tazilites was that the Qur'an was not uncreated as the traditionalists argued, but created, and therefore subject to the critique of human reason. It sounds perhaps like so much hair splitting, but it had the import of Christian theological debate around the divinity and humanity of Jesus. Basing all their arguments on reason (doing theology from below, one could say), the Mu'tazilites believed that taking such texts as the Throne Verse literally made no sense at all; for the anthropomorphism thus entailed would bring God down to human scale. It was simply not rational to speak that way about the transcendent. In his classic Mu'tazilite commentary, Zamakhshari says of the *kursi* or footstool attached to the Throne: "It is no more than an image expressing God's greatness. In reality, there is neither *kursi,* an act of sitting, nor one who sits."[9] The verse therefore uses a "fanciful image" to communicate the idea of God's extensive power, knowledge, and sovereignty.[10]

Al-Ash'ari had been a member of the Mu'tazilites in his youth and became disaffected with their inability to rein in their own rational arguments. He countered that, on the contrary, what made no sense was any attempt to limit God in any direction whatsoever. He concluded that one simply ought not speculate about what God has in mind. If the Qur'an says God sits on a Throne, one must take the statement at face value and let it be. He quotes with utmost approval the Hadith of Muhammad, "The *kursi* is the place of the two feet (the footstool of God). It has a squeaking sound like that of a new saddle."[11] His now famous methodological formula *bila kayf* ("without a how") sums up his conviction that theorizing is counter-productive. Ash'ari's opinion has carried the day, for the most part, with its emphasis on divine mystery.

The Shi'a or Shi'ite Muslims were especially partial to still another type of exegesis. Just as the jurists read scripture with an eye for regulatory items and the rationalists went for the anthropomorphisms, Shi'ite interpreters have been keen to focus on any text that might support the religious and political legitimacy of Muhammad's son-in-law Ali and his descendants. Shi'ite exegesis is therefore highly allegorical. Recall, for example, the Verse of Light. One classic reading of it likens God's light to Muhammad, the niche to Muhammad's breast, the lamp to the knowledge of prophecy, the glass to Muhammad's prophetic knowledge passed along to Ali. That the tree is neither of east nor west means Ali was neither Jew nor Christian. Just as the tree nearly glowed even untouched by fire, so Ali would nearly utter the prophetic knowledge even if Muhammad had not passed it on. And the phrase "Light upon light" refers to the succession of one Imam (spiritual descendant of Ali) from the previous Imam.[12]

Finally, one can speak also of a mystical type of exegesis. Islamic mystics have read the sacred text for any hint of the possibility of an intimate relationship between human and

Key Concepts

Aya(t): A "verse" of the Qur'an; a "sign" of God in the created world.

Hadith: "Tradition, Sayings" of Muhammad, second in authority only to the Qur'an.

Hajj: (Major) Pilgrimage to Makka during the pilgrimage month, twelfth of the lunar year.

Hijra: Muhammad's "emigration" from Makka to Madina in 622 C.E. marking the beginning of Islamic history.

Ijma': "Consensus" of the community with regard to the application of the revealed law.

Jihad: "Striving, struggle" in the way of God, including religiously sanctioned warfare.

Madhhab: A school of Islamic jurisprudence or legal methodology.

Minaret: A tall, slender tower attached to a mosque from which the call to prayer emanates.

Mi'raj: "Ascension" of Muhammad into Heaven; metaphor for spiritual journey.

Mujahidin: Persons who partake in *jihad*, whether physical or spiritual.

Qibla: The "direction" of Makka, toward which one turns in prayer and spiritual readiness.

Salat: The technical term for the ritual prayer offered five times daily.

Shahada: Profession of faith: There is no god but God, Muhammad is the messenger of God.

Shari'a: The "Main Road" along which Muslim's walk as a community; by extension, all of divinely revealed Law.

Shirk: Setting up partners or associates with God; idolatry.

Sunna: "Way of life," normative example of Muhammad transmitted largely in the Hadith.

Tawhid: The acknowledgment and assertion of the oneness and transcendence of God.

Ulama: Class of persons who are "learned" in religious matters, religious scholars.

Umma: The global community of Muslims.

Umra: (Lesser) Pilgrimage to Makka, often performed outside of formal Pilgrimage month.

divine. Traditionalists often found such talk at least slightly blasphemous, and rationalists regarded it as sentimental at best. But the rich mystical tradition has mined every reference to divine love and concern, every suggestion of divine immanence, discerning at least two levels of meaning in each tidbit. The outward meaning is apparent to most everyone; to arrive at the hidden meaning requires *ta'wil,* the very thing some would say the Qur'an counsels against (Qur'an 3:7 quoted above).

Some examples of the Qur'anic phrases dearest to the mystics include the following: "To God belong the East and the West; wherever you turn, there is the face of God" (2:115); "I am truly near: I answer the prayer of the petitioner who beseeches me. Therefore let them respond to me and have faith in me, that they might receive guidance" (2:186); "Everything on earth perishes; but the face of your Lord remains, majestic and most revered" (55:26–27). While the mystical tradition was not loath to interpret such texts metaphorically, they did so without in any way deflating them of their mystery as the Mu'tazilite approach ran the risk of doing. In his reading of the Throne Verse, for example, the mystic Ibn Arabi considers the *kursi* to be the center of knowledge on the cosmic scale as is the human heart on the microcosmic level. He goes on to say that God does not tire of keeping all things in existence "because they have no existence without Him. . . . Rather the realm of the ideal form is His inner dimension and the realm of forms is His outer dimension. They have no existence except in Him. Nor are they other than He."[13] Such statements as the last, liable as it may seem to the charge of pantheistic monism, were the sort of utterances for which many a mystic ran afoul of more traditional thinkers.

Before we move on to the Prophet, two other beautiful short texts will help to reinforce the sense of power and inexhaustible grandeur Muslims experience in their scripture.

The first text and its parallel emphasize the infinitude of God's revelation, extending impossibly beyond creation's capacity: "If all the trees on earth were pens and all the oceans ink, with seven more seas besides, they would not suffice to record the words of God." (Qur'an 31:27, see also 18:109) Christian readers may be reminded of the text with which John's Gospel ends: "But there are so many other things which Jesus did; were every one of them to be written, I suppose that the world itself could not contain the books that would be written."[14] The second is reminiscent of a theme associated with Mount Sinai. When God gave Moses the Torah, Sinai swooned; according to the mystics and rabbis, it exploded into many pieces, each of which fell upon and blessed a part of the earth. "If we had sent this Qur'an down upon a mountain, you would have seen it crumble to pieces and humble itself for fear of God." (Qur'an 59:21)

Muhammad and the History of Prophethood

> Say "We believe in God and what has been revealed to us and what was revealed to Abraham and Isma'il and Isaac and Jacob and the tribes, and what was given to Moses and Jesus and what was given to the prophets from their Lord. We make no distinction among them and to Him do we surrender gratefully (lit. we are Muslims to Him). (Qur'an 2:136; see also 29:46)

Jewish and Christian readers will already have some familiarity with the notion of prophets and prophetic mission. Since time immemorial, prophet-types have played a major role in the religious history of the Middle East. In the Hebrew scriptures, prophets receive a mandate to speak on God's behalf. Their mission often requires that they stand up to the high and mighty, posing the divine challenge of justice for the powerless of the earth. The problem of how to discern true prophets from charlatans has exercised religious minds for millennia as well. In addition to the full-fledged prophets, lesser characters have also played a part. These include sages, oracles and soothsayers.

All of these religious types were familiar to many people in the Arabia of Muhammad's day. But as Muhammad would discover, the majority of the populace welcomed the advent of a prophet no more enthusiastically in the seventh century C.E. than they would have in the seventh century B.C.E. A brief summary of the major events of Muhammad's life will provide the necessary immediate context for our consideration of his paradigmatic role in the life of the Muslim community.

Muhammad was born in the trading town of Makka around 570 C.E. to a rather poor family of the clan of Hashim, one of the branches of the Quraysh tribe. His father died before Muhammad was born and the boy's mother died when he was six years old. According to Arabian custom, the youngster was sent to be reared among the Bedouin. Tradition names his nurse Halima. After his mother's death, Muhammad grew up in the custody first of grandfather Abd al-Muttalib and later in the house of his uncle Abu Talib, whose son Ali we have already mentioned briefly and who will return in Chapter 3. Tradition has it that the young Muhammad traveled with his uncle on business. One story tells how in Syria they met an old Christian monk named Bahira, who discerned the marks of prophetic greatness in the boy.

When Muhammad was about twenty-five, he married a widow fifteen years his senior. Khadija ran her own caravan business, and Muhammad went to work for her. Apparently Muhammad liked occasionally to retreat to mountain solitude to meditate and seek within the source of life. Around

610 C.E., when Muhammad had reached the age long considered in the Middle East a necessary precondition for the imparting of wisdom and ministry, he began to experience troubling visitations that sent him in turmoil to ask Khadija's counsel.

On the "Night of Power" now commemorated on the 27th of Ramadan, the earliest message commanded him to "Recite!" (Qur'an 96:1; lit. "make qur'an") that which no human being could know unaided. The encounter left him confused and uncertain. Not until as much as a year later did Muhammad hear a follow-up message of confirmation: "Indeed your Lord is the one who best knows who has strayed from His path, who best knows those who are guided." (Qur'an 68:7) Assured that he was not losing his sanity, Muhammad persisted in his attitude of attentiveness to the messages from the unseen world. From then on revelations came more frequently. During the next several years, Muhammad slowly gathered a circle of "converts" who would form the nucleus of a faith community. Leaders of the Quraysh grew increasingly unhappy at the effects of Muhammad's preaching on caravan and pilgrim traffic to the Ka'ba and at the prospect of a rival leader in their midst. Around 615 C.E., under growing pressure and amid threats to the safety of his community, Muhammad sent a group off to seek asylum across the Red Sea with the Christian ruler of Abyssinia (Ethiopia). Muhammad remained in Makka.

Tradition reports that on the 27th night of the month of Rajab in the year 621 C.E., Muhammad underwent a twofold mystical experience. In the first part, God "carried his servant by night, from the Mosque of the Sanctuary to the Farther Mosque." (Qur'an 17:1) Later interpreters would equate the first site with the shrine of the Ka'ba in Makka, the second with the southern end of the temple platform in Jerusalem, where now stands an early eighth century structure called "the Farther Mosque" (*al-masjid al-aqsa*). This "Night Journey" (*isra'*) was already clearly a kind of otherworldly experience, for ancient narratives place Muhammad in the company of earlier prophets in the Farther Mosque, and they naturally ask him to lead them in the ritual prayer. The second phase of the journey, however, called the "Ascension" (*mi'raj*), finds the Prophet riding a winged human-faced steed named Buraq and led by Gabriel toward the very throne of God. Marvelously embellished tales have developed around this experience. Vivid descriptions of Muhammad's excursion follow him through the various levels of heaven, where he meets all of his major prophetic forebears, down to the dark circles of hell where Gabriel shows him the horrors of the damned. This is truly the picture of an heroic journey of initiation in the mysteries of the unseen world. Many Muslims believe the journey involved physical locomotion, but a strong tradition of non-literalistic interpretation has always regarded it as a spiritual and inward experience. We shall return to this experience in Chapter 4 to consider it as a paradigm of the individual Muslim's spiritual path.

During the year of the Night Journey and Ascension, and perhaps also during the previous year, Muhammad had been investigating the possibility of moving his community from the increasingly hostile environment of Makka to a safer haven. Hopeful prospects arrived in 621 C.E. with a delegation from Yathrib, a city several hundred miles north of Makka. Looking for someone to help them negotiate a peaceful settlement to factional problems in their city, the representatives invited Muhammad to come and apply his already renowned talent for arbitration. Arrangements were finalized, and in 622 C.E. the Muslims headed north to Yathrib, whose name would soon change to Madinat an-Nabi ("City of the Prophet"), or simply Madina. That crucial journey was called the Hijra or Emigration. It marked the birthday of Islam, so to speak, and the beginning of the Muslim calendar (with dates marked A.H., "after the Hijra"). Chapter 2 will discuss this journey further, as it developed in Islamic piety and as a metaphor for the Muslim community's relationship with the world at large.

Muhammad's years in Madina, as reflected in the text of the Qur'an as well as in later historical writing, witnessed major changes in his style of leadership and in the shape of the community of believers. Muhammad's prominence in the new setting gave prestige to the community. As the group increased, so did the demands on Muhammad's administrative time and skill, so that what began as spiritual leadership gradually grew into a more comprehensive oversight. During the Madinan period the Muslims also took up arms against the Quraysh and fought a number of serious military engagements with the Makkan forces. After nearly eight years of bitter conflict, the two sides struck a truce. The Muslims would be allowed to return to Makka without opposition. In 630 Muhammad led a triumphal band to claim the city for the Muslims. Two years later Muhammad returned to Makka for what would be his farewell pilgrimage to the Ka'ba. Chapter 3 will consider the Hajj again, as a religious symbol and experience of return to the center, and as a metaphor around which to understand Islam as a unique community of faith.

Given this brief overview of the key events in Muhammad's life, it remains for us to try to understand how Muhammad saw himself within the larger sweep of God's use of prophets to reveal the Word to humankind. Both the Qur'an and the Hadith (Traditions or sayings attributed to Muhammad) are replete with references to earlier prophets, from Adam to Jesus. Islamic tradition numbers over two dozen figures sent to particular peoples, including David, Solomon, Noah, and Jonah, as well as the Arabian figures Hud, Salih, and Shu'ayb. All of them are "prophets" (*nabi,* pl. *anbiya'*) commissioned to warn their people; some are in addition "messengers" (*rasul,* pl. *rusul*) to whom scriptures are revealed. All of the prophets and messengers experienced rejection at the hands of their people, and some were killed. In every instance, God dealt harshly with the people.

Muhammad readily identified with several of the prophets in particular, especially with Abraham, the "Friend of the Merciful" (*Khalil ar-Rahman*), and with Moses, "God's Conversant" (*Kalim Allah*). In Islamic tradition, Abraham was neither Jew nor Christian, but a *hanif,* a seeker after the one true God. As the Qur'an says:

> Truly Abraham was a model (lit. an *umma*), obedient to God, and a seeker (lit. *hanif*) who assigned no partner to God. He responded in gratitude to the bounty of the one who chose him and guided him to the Straight Path. . . . So We have revealed to you (Muhammad) that you should follow the believing ways (lit. *milla*) of Abraham the seeker. . . . (Qur'an 16:120–21, 123)

It was Abraham who had prayed that God would "send among them a messenger from their midst who will unfold to them your signs and teach them the Book and the wisdom." (Qur'an 2:129)

Moses' importance in the Qur'an is equal to that of Abraham. "We sent Moses with Our signs: 'Bring your people out from profound darkness into the light and make them mindful of the days of God.' Truly in that are signs for all who are long-suffering and grateful." (Qur'an 4:5) Qur'an 73:15 likens Muhammad especially to Moses. Islamic tradition likewise sees a reference to Muhammad in the words of Deuteronomy 18:18, in which God says to Moses, "I will raise up for them a prophet like you from among their kinsmen, and will put my words in his mouth; he shall tell them all that I command him."[15] Curiously, one text of the Qur'an (7:155–57) has God speaking approvingly to Moses of "those who follow the Apostle, the unlettered Prophet (i.e. Muhammad) whom they find written of (in their own) Torah and Gospel. . . ." The allusion is apparently first to the text of Deuteronomy just mentioned, and secondly to references in John 14–16 to the Paraclete.

Medieval Muslim theologians interpreted the Johannine text in a fascinating manner. Here comes that second Arabic lesson. Speakers of Semitic languages such as Arabic become accustomed to find basic meanings in consonantal roots of words that, when written, are without vowels. Transferring that way of thinking to Greek, scholars reasoned that Christians had misread Jesus' term as *parakletos,* "Advocate or counselor," interpreted by Christians as the Holy Spirit. A simple insertion of the correct vowels would yield *periklutos,* "the highly praised one," and thus a meaning more acceptable to Muslims. The name Muhammad in Arabic derives from the root *HaMaDa,* "to praise." When Arabic wants to intensify a root meaning, it doubles the middle consonant, hence *HaMMaDa,* "to praise highly." In order to express the idea that a particular individual has been praised highly, Arabic forms a passive participle by prefixing *mu-* and producing the word *muHaMMaD,* the "highly praised one."

What is most important to note in all this is the Muslim conviction that God sends a message to suit every circumstance perfectly. As the Qur'an says, "We [God] have sent no messenger except with the language of his people, that he might give them clarity. God allows to wander off whom He will, and He guides whom He will." (Qur'an 4:4)

All prophets have been wayfarers, as have all human beings. But what distinguishes prophets, from Adam to Muhammad, from the rest of wandering humankind is that God's messengers come on the explicit mission of helping the rest find their way amid the confusion, the maze of possible paths and goals, the plethora of markers and way-stations. Islamic tradition offers a wide range of imaginative models of spiritual progress. One model associates various stages along the way with individual prophet-guides. The latter are in turn associated with particular colors, degrees of spiritual achievement, levels of the cosmos, and such human faculties as heart, spirit, and innermost secret. Using such a model, one can speak of spiritual progress as a process of encountering a succession of the "prophets of one's own being" as the traveler proceeds upward through the spectrum of colors and from the gross to the subtle.[16]

A Note on Journey Imagery in Its Arabic-Islamic Context

Before we embark on our excursion through the world of Islam on the trail blazed by the Prophet, it will be instructive to have some idea about the semantic foundation of our use of journey imagery. It is surely a common metaphor, but there are solid linguistic reasons why it seems especially close to the heart of Islamic tradition and particularly expressive of Muslim aspirations.

It is by no means incidental that Muslims regard Arabic as the language of divine revelation. Arabic is therefore the tradition's "canonical" language. Even among Muslims who have no working knowledge of Arabic, its thought patterns and vocabulary have had enormous impact. Converts to Islam in the United States regularly take Arabic names, for example. Within Arabic's very rich lexicon one finds a number of words with significant directional or spatial connotations. A word commonly used for "perception or understanding" comes from a root meaning "to catch up with" (*iDRaK,* from the root *DaRaKa*—here the upper case letters indicate the tri-consonantal root which Arabic shares with all Semitic languages such as Hebrew). One of the most commonly used words for "to know" (*'aLiMa*) shares its triliteral root with words for "world, cosmos" (*'aLaM*) and "marker, sign-post" (*'aLaM*). A term used to refer to the biography or life story of Muhammad (*SiRa*) is rooted in the verb "to travel, move along" (*SARa*). The most common Arabic term for "heart" (*QaLB*) comes from the same root as words for "to turn around, conversion, return, center" (*QaLaBa, inQiLaB*).

A number of terms also bear a more explicitly religious or theological significance. *SHaRi'a,* the single most important term for the whole of divine revelation, including law and practice elaborated from Qur'an and the sayings of Muhammad, also means "oasis, source of water," and derives from a root meaning "to set out for" the watering hole (*SHaRa'a*). Finally, a term used in reference both to the way of life pursued by an individual seeker after God and to formally structured religious orders (*TaRiQa*) is usually translated as "path."

I do not mean to suggest that even native speakers of Arabic are always conscious of the spatial or directional connotations of terms with such intriguing subliminals. However, those complex associations remain an integral part of the Islamic heritage. All of life truly is a journey through the "Two Worlds." A Muslim who lives in faith travels in and beyond space and time, and "catches up with" the inner and outer meanings of creation through a "conversion of heart" that leads to the ultimate oasis, the Water of Life.

Questions for Discussion

1. With what images of God from Judaism, Christianity, Hinduism or Native American traditions, for example, might one compare central Islamic images of God? How can a reli-

gious person's images of God influence the individual's overall approach to life? How can the notion of divine names offer insight into Islam and other traditions?

2. Find parallels in Jewish, Christian, Hindu, Buddhist or Chinese sacred texts to the Qur'an's Throne Verse and Verse of Light.

3. Discuss the following Hadith: Abu Sa'id al-Khudri reported God's Messenger as saying that Moses asked his Lord to teach him something with which to make mention of Him or to supplicate Him, and was told to say, "There is no god but God." He [Moses] replied to his Lord that all His servants said this, but he wanted something particularly for himself, and He [God] said, "Moses, were the seven heavens and their inhabitants apart from me and the seven earths put in one side of a balance and 'There is no god but God' in the other, 'There is no god but God' would outweigh them."[17]

4. Discuss parallels between Qur'anic and Biblical images of Joseph of Egypt, Abraham, Moses, Jesus and Mary.

5. How in general has Muhammad's life served as an exemplar for Muslims?

2

Hijra: Signs on the Horizons and Striving in the Way of God

In this chapter we look at Islam as a global religious culture and in its relationships to the world around itself. We begin with Muhammad's exemplary journey away from home, the Hijra, as a model for the Muslim's encounter with the world outside the abode of Islam. Then we discuss questions that arise with respect to Islam as part of the human community, in relation to other religious traditions, and finally as the broader cultural contribution of Muslims. All of these issues we situate within the context of the Islamic conviction that all of creation possesses revelatory power and that human beings must learn to read God's "Signs on the Horizons."

Hijra as a Metaphor for Life as "Striving in the Way of God" (*Jihad fi sabil Allah*)

One can look at the notion of Hijra from at least three points of view. Hijra's first and foremost meaning for Muslims is the Prophet's historic move with the first *muhajirun* in 622 C.E. Second, Hijra can refer to the physical recapitulation of Muhammad's migration as performed by countless Muslims over the last fourteen hundred years. According to one Muslim author,

> The Muslim scholars not only look at the *Hijrah* from a religious and historical perspective, but also consider it in

Timeline of Major Events and Developments

570:	Birth of Muhammad
595:	Muhammad's marriage to Khadija, mother of Fatima
610:	Initial revelation of Qur'an to Muhammad through Angel Gabriel
622:	Hijra, emigration of Muslim community from Makka to Madina
632:	Muhammad's death
632–661:	Period of the "Rightly Guided Caliphs," first successors to Muhammad
661–750:	Period of the Umayyad Dynasty, capital at Damascus, major expansion as far as Spain and India; gradual development of Shi'ite Islam following death of Ali
750–1258:	Period of the Abbasid Dynasty, capital at Baghdad, gradual breakdown into regional political entities from Spain to India
750–900:	Formation of the four major Sunni schools of religious law, major developments in Qur'anic exegetical sciences, canonization of the Hadith literature
1099–1189:	First Crusade and Latin Kingdom of Jerusalem, ended by Saladin
1189–1290:	Muslim responses to subsequent major Crusades leave Muslims in control of most of the central Middle East
1100–1400:	Growth and spread of major Sufi brotherhoods from Iberia to Indonesia
1111:	Death of Abu Hamid al-Ghazali, influential religious thinker and author
1198:	Death of Ibn Rushd (Averroes), famed Iberian-born philosopher
1210–1526:	Delhi Sultanates, powerful Muslim presence in India
1250–1517:	Mamluk dynasty in Egypt and central Middle East
1258:	Mongols destroy Baghdad, ending the Abbasid Dynasty
1300–1921:	Ottoman Dynasty rules Turkey and much of the eastern Mediterranean
1526–1757:	Mughal Dynasty rules much of India
1791:	Death of Muhammad ibn Abd al-Wahhab, founder of Wahhabi movement in Arabian peninsula
1849–1905:	Life of Muhammad Abduh, proponent of reason as source of knowledge
1865–1935:	Rashid Rida, founder of Egyptian Salafi movement calling for retrieval of pristine days of the Prophet
1922–24:	Mustafa Kemal Ataturk secularizes Turkish state
1906–49:	Life of Hasan al-Banna, whose Muslim Brotherhood (1929) gains strength with failure of liberal Muslim governments and proclamation of the State of Israel
1909–66:	Life of Sayyid Qutb, influential theorist of Muslim Brotherhood movement
1947:	Partition of India creates Muslim state of Pakistan
1979:	Islamic Republic of Iran proclaimed after overthrow of last Shah
2002:	Global Muslim population reaches 1.2 billion

a wider context as a phenomenon in the religio-social life of Muslims which has been repeatedly recurring since the time of the Prophet to the present day. Whenever it was found impossible by any group of devout Muslims to worship Allah in totality and follow the way of Islam freely in all its aspects and dimensions, they performed *Hijrah* to a place where it was possible to accomplish this objective in their life.[1]

Third, Hijra can have a still broader metaphorical connotation. It can refer to a wide range of acts and relationships that, while not involving a literal migration, define the Islamic tradition's ways of dealing with the world. Chapter 1 explored the first level of meaning; here we discuss several dimensions of the term's other meanings.

Long before Muhammad heard the call to "emigrate" with his young community from Makka to Madina, other prophets had set the example. Insecurity, risk, and utter trust in God form the core of the prophetic vocation, and *hijra* (from *HaJaRa* meaning to separate, leave behind) marks but the first step in the prophet's lifelong journey. According to Islamic tradition, Abraham left home for the unknown, forsaking his father's idol carving shop, on his way to Makka where God ordered him to build the Ka'ba. Jealous brothers separated the young Joseph from his grieving father; before he could be elevated to lordship and return to Jacob, Joseph had to endure the "Well of Separation." Before Moses could be commissioned to lead the people of Israel he had to flee Egypt for the land of Midian. Before he could claim Makka in the name of Islam, Muhammad had to relinquish it.

Muhammad's Hijra began to acquire paradigmatic status fairly early in Islamic history. Two traditions from a popular anthology of *hadith,* sayings of the Prophet, offer some important clues. In the first, one of the Companions (a technical term for a member of the first generation of Muslims) asks Muhammad a series of questions about faith. He wants to know specifically what are the "most excellent" aspects of certain Muslim beliefs and practices. Asked about the Hijra, Muhammad explains that its essential meaning lay in "abandoning what your Lord abhors." Migration has clearly begun to mean something more than mere physical relocation.

Elsewhere in the anthology, various sayings apocalyptic in tone depict Muhammad warning his people to prepare for the dissension and turmoil that will arise as time nears its end. That process of spiritual entropy will impose serious hardships and test every believer's commitment to religious observance. "The reward for engaging in worship during the turmoil," the Prophet explains, "will be like that for coming to me as emigrants." Those who remain steadfast when people all around seem to be abandoning values will reap the spiritual rewards of the very Muslims who made the original Hijra with Muhammad himself. The Prophet's emigration has thus become a kind of standard by which to measure religious merit.[2]

Several centuries later, during the flowering of Islamic religious poetry especially in Arabic and Persian, the mystics developed the theme further. Persian poet Jalal ad-Din Rumi (d. 1273) chose to develop a single small detail of the story of the Hijra into a metaphor for the relationship between the (human) Lover and the (divine) Beloved. When the Hijra began, Muhammad sent the Muslims north in small groups, while he and several companions remained till all else had departed. Muhammad then left with Abu Bakr. Along the way, they took refuge in a cave from the pursuing Quraysh, concealed there by the spider God inspired to spin its web across the opening. Rumi calls Muhammad and Abu Bakr, together in the earth as though in a single heart, the "Friends of the Cave." Abu Bakr the spiritual aspirant sits at the feet of

Muhammad the master, the *shaykh,* the spiritual guide. Rumi and other mystics therefore think of Hijra as a crucial phase in every seeker's development. Like Abu Bakr the seeker must stay with the Prophet through moments of the most terrifying detachment.[3]

In more recent times, Muslims all over the world continue to employ the vocabulary of Hijra to express important aspects of their value systems. In the Middle East an organization is known as *Takfir wa Hijra* ("Atonement/accusation of infidelity and Hijra"); this name uses the metaphor to describe its desire to revive traditional values and re-Islamicize their world. In Southeast Asia, some Muslims consider symbolic Hijra an ongoing possibility. Anyone who leaves home in search of education or a place more conducive to the practice of Islam gains blessings equal to those the first *muhajirun* won when they accompanied Muhammad to Madina.[4]

A verse from the Qur'an has provided an occasion for fascinating commentary and further elaboration on the need to leave behind the familiar and comfortable to confront the evil in oneself and in one's world.

> Whoever leaves home [literally, makes hijra] in God's cause will find on the earth frequent and ample place of refuge. If death should overtake the one who leaves home and migrates to God and His Messenger, God is certain to reward that person. (Qur'an 4:100)

No less a figure than Imam Ruhallah Khumayni offers some intriguing suggestions as to how contemporary Muslims should understand the text. In a psychological reading of "home" as "selfhood" or self-centeredness, Khumayni writes:

> If a person departs from the home of egohood and migrates toward God and His Messenger [migrating to the

Messenger being a form of migrating toward God], and then reaches a state where he is "overtaken by death," where nothing remains of his self and he sees all things as coming from God—if he engages in such a migration, then it is incumbent upon God to reward him. . . . There is a class of people who have accomplished this. . . . There are others who have migrated but not yet reached the goal of being "overtaken by death." And there is still another group—to which you and I belong—that has not even begun to migrate. We are still caught up in darkness; we are captives in the pit of attachment to the world [evidently an allusion to Joseph in the well—author], to nature, and worst of all, to our own egos. We are enclosed in our home of selfhood, and all that exists is for ourselves. . . . As time goes on, we become more and more distant from our point of origin, that place toward which we are supposed to migrate.[5]

Hijra thus simultaneously involves leaving the comfort of the familiar and setting out toward what is paradoxically both unknown and, given sufficient trust, a sure success.

Khumayni has implicitly combined here two key elements of Islamic spirituality, Hijra and the "Greater Jihad," or struggle against one's tendencies to self-centeredness. We shall return to the latter concept in Chapter 4, and to its flipside, the "Lesser Jihad" against external injustice and evil shortly in the present chapter. In any case, an essential prerequisite to Hijra is the destruction of one's cherished idols. Few stories exemplify that more effectively than the Qur'an's account of how Abraham severed his ties to home and family in his search for a new direction in life. One night, the scripture says, Abraham beheld a star and said: This is my Lord. But when the star vanished, he corrected himself, saying: I love not things that set. When the moon rose, Abraham exclaimed: This must be my Lord. But when it, too, set, he said:

Were not my Lord guiding me, I would surely be among the lost. And when he saw the sun come up he said: This must indeed be my Lord, for it is greater by far. But when the sun went down, Abraham addressed his father's people: Far be it from me to set up partners with God as you do.

Abraham thus began his Hijra. In the following verse, the Qur'an has Abraham say the words every Muslim says at the start of the ritual prayer as they face Makka: "I have turned my face toward Him who created heavens and earth (i.e. not to created nature itself), as a seeker after the One God, in grateful surrender (literally as a *hanif* and a *muslim*), and I worship none but God." (Qur'an 6:76–79). Abraham could face the true center of life only after he had eliminated all that could compete for his attention. Such is the meaning of Hijra in the lives of millions of Muslims: reading the "signs on the horizons" for what they reveal of God, and dealing with the facts of life in this world. To those who refuse to make the Hijra, the Qur'an addresses the words:

> I will turn away from my signs those who walk proudly on earth. Though they see every sign, they will put no credence in them. Though they may see the way of uprightness they will not set out upon it. Should they see the errant way, that they will claim as theirs; for they denied and refused to attend to our signs. (Qur'an 7:146)

Signs on the Horizons

> Behold, in the heavens and the earth are signs for those who believe. And in your creation, and all the wild creatures He has scattered over the earth, are signs for a people of firm faith. And the alternation of night and day, and the sustenance that God sends down from the sky, to revive the earth after its death, and the shifting of the

winds—these are signs for a people who understand. . . .
Here is vision for humankind, guidance and mercy. . . .
(Qur'an 45:3–5, 20)

Creation, extending to the limits of heaven and earth as
suggested by the term "horizons," is the "terrain" on which
Muslims journey, along with the rest of humankind. God's
handiwork appears often in the Qur'an as the first, if not the
foremost, locus of divine revelation. It comes down to this:
anyone who sees the natural world in all its wonder with open
eyes and an open heart will see there the unmistakable signs
of the Creator. Islam comes nowhere near to pantheism. The
difference between God and creation is infinite; one discerns
divinity through nature rather than precisely in nature. As
human beings begin to acknowledge God's creativity, they
respond naturally in gratitude and in a variety of natural symbols, a creation-inspired language. A "Sacred Hadith," a tradition attributed to God rather than to Muhammad, says: "I
was a hidden treasure and I desired to be known, so I created
the world." Knowing God through that world renders all
created beings naturally "muslim," for all non-human things
by nature surrender to God. As the Qur'an says not long after
the Verse of Light, "Do you not see that it is God whom all in
heaven and on earth, and the birds in formation, praise?
Every being knows its proper prayer and praise." (Qur'an
24:41, with the word for "prayer" being *salat,* the technical
term for ritual prayer) Only human beings have to choose
whether they will prefer self-centeredness and the illusion
of control.

People who willingly surrender in gratitude ("islam")
tend more or less spontaneously to express their response in
ritual and symbol that are both uniquely their own and common to all other religious persons. Chapter 3 will take up the
distinctively Islamic dimensions of these religious expres-

sions; here, borrowing concepts from the phenomenology of religion, we look briefly at some aspects of ritual and symbol that form a bond between Muslims and non-Muslims alike. Ritual and symbol are ways all religious people externalize their acknowledgment of the signs on the horizons, and through which they effect a right relationship to the cosmos.

Almost all religious traditions recommend fasting in some form or other. Islamic practice retains a particularly rigorous version of the seasonal fast during the ninth lunar month of Ramadan, which is movable in relation to solar reckoning and thus rotates through the solar year. Abstaining from food, drink, and sexual gratification from dawn to sunset every day (sometimes as long as eighteen hours or more) for thirty days breaks the ordinary pattern of life as a sharp reminder to consider dimensions of life to which one would otherwise rarely attend. Refraining from ordinary recourse to creation's sustenance requires a discipline that is capable of reminding the individual of a greater need that creation cannot assuage. Not alone from physical goods does one fast, but from a range of physical and spiritual evils as well. The latter include the likes of envy and hatred, along with such lesser faults as a tendency to complain or cut corners in work. Among the desired effects of the practice Muslims count a deepened compassion for people all too familiar with hunger, a heightened capacity to counter one's own baser tendencies (what we have referred to as the Greater Jihad), and a clearer sense of one's relationship to the Creator.

Fasting's dimension of social awareness connects it to the practice of almsgiving, also common to, or at least recommended by, virtually all religious traditions. Again, Muslims have maintained a somewhat more systematic form of the practice than have most branches of either Judaism or Christianity, although ritual "tithing" is still strong in some churches. One of the lessons of creation's signs is that human beings do not own natural riches permanently; we merely borrow them. The same holds for other forms of wealth. Muslim tradition recommends that believers "give God a loan" and "spend in the way of God" as a way of caring for creation and sharing what they have received. The term *zakat* originally derives from a root that means "to purify oneself," in this case, of the illusion of ownership. God alone is substantially and eternally wealthy. The point of giving alms, like that of fasting, is to remind the donor of the source of all good gifts, rather than to give that warm feeling that comes from self-congratulation. In the Qur'an's words:

> Give to kin, the poor and the traveler what they need; that is best for those who seek the face of God, and they will indeed fare well. What you give in the hope of profiting at the expense of people will gain you nothing in God's sight; what you give in the form of alms (lit. *zakat*) as you seek the face of God—that will produce abundant return. (Qur'an 30:38–39)

Related to the purification that almsgiving both requires and fosters is the sort of ritual ablution many traditions consider a prerequisite to formal prayer. Water, a universal symbol of cleansing, provides the physical medium for Muslims as they wash before the five daily prayers. The tradition makes it clear that the purification is at least as much spiritual as it is bodily; if water is not available, one can use sand or even earth to wipe over the feet, forearms, and so forth. The requirements are thus far from literalistic. Purification functions primarily as an embodiment of the praying person's movement into a sacred time.

Right relation to the cosmos also involves recognition that entering a sacred time means marking off and entering sacred space. Traditional societies still preserve a strong sense of sacred geography, considering architectural siting and orientation at least as important as building materials. Christian churches were once always built facing the rising sun, synagogues facing Jerusalem. The exigencies of real estate availability, along with a broad range of distractions from the ancient sense of being rooted in the earth, have all but wiped out the vestiges of cosmic orientation in many religious communities. Islamic tradition has maintained a firmly grounded conviction of a spiritual center, a symbolic *axis mundi,* a place at which heaven meets earth and from which all creation radiates. That place is Makka in the west-central Arabian peninsula. Whenever Muslims pray liturgically, whether alone or in congregation at noon on Friday, they turn toward Makka as suggested in the Qur'anic text cited in Chapter 1 (2:144). Chapter 4 will treat the matter of individual or non-liturgical prayer.

Pilgrimage is the final dimension of sacred space among religious persons the world over. Like other ritual acknowledgments of sacred space and time, the practice of pilgrimage has fallen off in less traditional societies such as our own. India and even Japan are home to innumerable sites to which pilgrims still travel in large numbers. Chances are that if any of us cared to ask, we would find traces of some once-frequented local pilgrimage site within a half-day drive from our homes. Of all the world's religious traditions, none has maintained so strong a sense of its members as a community on pilgrimage as has the Islamic tradition. Given good health and sufficient means, Muslims are enjoined to visit Makka at least once during the sacred time of pilgrimage, the Hajj. Muslims are welcome to come to Makka and Madina any time during the year, but fulfill formally the duty of Hajj only between the eighth and thirteenth days of the twelfth lunar month.

One of the most powerful symbols in the complex ritual

of the Hajj is the counterclockwise circumambulation (*tawaf*) of the Ka'ba. Practiced in many religious traditions, circumambulation represents a process of assimilation, of seeking to make something one's own. The process allows one sometimes to receive spiritual power, as in the case of pilgrimage; sometimes to exert power, as in the case of Joshua's legendary siege of Jericho; sometimes to hallow and reverence, as in the case of Christian procession around a church or a Hindu's final commendation of a loved one's mortal remains on the funeral pyre. Pilgrimage symbolism, from change of garb to the cutting of a lock of hair to the removal of all indicators of social or economic privilege, expresses outwardly the pilgrim's desire for a change of heart and mind. Chapter 3 will discuss Hajj as a metaphor for the return to the center as well as the particulars of pilgrimage myth and ritual.

Islam and the Human Community

Dimensions of Striving in the Way of God

With that background on the prophetic paradigm of Hijra and on Islam in the context of the global history of religion, we turn to a number of particular issues that face Muslims and all humankind as members of the human community. These include environmental concerns, economics, justice and peace, human rights, and interreligious relations. In so small a space one can hope only to mention some of the larger questions; our purpose here is not to solve any of these immense problems, but merely to provide a sense of what Islamic sources seem to recommend in dealing with them.

Set out, then, accoutered lightly or heavily, and strive (literally, engage in jihad) with your possessions and your selves in the way of God. That is best for you, if only you knew. Had their compensation been swift and the journey undemanding, they would surely have followed you (Muhammad); but they found the long haul arduous. (Qur'an 9:41–2)

From an historical perspective, Muhammad's Hijra had enormous implications for the Muslim community's external relations. The Qur'an's Makkan suras, revealed prior to the Hijra of 622 C.E., speak of the jihad against one's lower tendencies, the Greater Jihad. When the Madinan suras use the term jihad, they seem generally to mean the Lesser Jihad. Muslims have therefore naturally associated the duty of hijra with that of struggle against outside enemies. Madina came to be known as the "Abode of Islam" (*dar al-islam*) as distinct from the "Abode of Unbelief/Idolatry/Conflict" (*dar al-kufr/shirk/ harb,* three variations used to describe the outside world). In addition to its generic sense of striving and struggle, jihad meant first of all the right of self-defense. Since the early Madinan community (initially numbering some five hundred in a city of about ten thousand) perceived itself under ongoing threat both from the Quraysh and their Makkan supporters, and from several tribal factions in and around Madina, jihad became a characteristic mode of relating to the non-Muslim world. The Qur'an emphasizes the defensive nature of any jihad involving military force (2:190).

Jihad has also carried from the earliest days a variety of meanings other than that associated with the use of violence. As one Muslim writer describes the situation, "Every sincere effort, however small and insignificant, and every struggle and sacrifice made in the way of Allah is termed as *Jihad* and this includes expressing the truth, enjoining right conduct, forbidding wrong actions, and sacrificing one's possessions and, if necessary, one's life in the way of Allah."[6] We turn now

to several crucial dimensions of religiously motivated
striving.

Islam and Environment

> Do they not see how each thing God has created, down to
> the very least, most humbly prostrates itself to God as its
> shadow revolves from the right and the left? To God all in
> heaven and on earth prostrates itself; from beasts to an-
> gels none withholds haughtily. In reverent fear of their
> transcendent Lord they do what they are bidden. (Qur'an
> 16:48–50)

Any discussion of religious attitudes toward the care and
keeping of our planet is bound to run head-on into the unpleasant fact that virtually no major religious community can
boast a very impressive record in implementing its stated values. Unfortunately, greed quickly swamps lofty but fragile
ideals in its wake. However unrealistic it may seem to speak of
a tradition's ideals without taking a hard look at how human
beings have actually behaved, ideals do need to be restated.
Our purpose here is neither to praise the Islamic community
uncritically for its environmental concerns nor to condemn
those Muslims who have played their part, along with the rest
of us, in sacrificing the earth on the altar of the great god
Profit.

In answer to the question of whether the Islamic tradition shares with Judaism and Christianity an appreciation of
the significance of creation, one can respond both affirma-
tively and negatively. Unlike the Bible, the Qur'an contains
no single integrated narrative of creation, suggests that God
would surely need no rest after his "work," and hints that a
"day" might actually be a very long time. In both sources
Adam is the first human being, but the Qur'an's descriptions

of the material vary from dust to semen to water to a clot of blood. Though the Qur'an's Adam also knows the names of all creatures, the emphasis is on God's knowledge rather than Adam's. In the Qur'anic stories, human beings are not created in God's image, for that would compromise the divine transcendence.

In general the Qur'an seems to place greater emphasis on God's sovereignty and power than does the biblical account. Whereas the Bible describes creation as a single original action, the Qur'an suggests that God is involved in creation as an ongoing activity, reasserting his creative prerogative with the emergence of each new living being. In the Bible, God seems to commission the first people unreservedly to take charge of the earth. Islamic tradition also regards the creation as given to humans to use, but God seems to hesitate a bit in turning the operation over to Adam and Eve. God offered to Heaven, Earth and the Mountains the "trust" of watching over creation. They declined out of fear, so God offered the Trust to humankind. Adam accepted, unjust and foolish as he was—and ungrateful in addition. When God informed his angels he was preparing to entrust creation to Adam as his representative (literally, caliph, vicegerent), they warned the Creator that human beings would surely act unjustly and violently. God assured the angels that the risk was worth taking. He had called forth from Adam's loins and assembled all of his yet unborn descendants and asked them, "Am I not your Lord?" They had responded as one and without hesitation, "Yes, we are witnesses to that!" (Qur'an 33:72, 2:30, 7:10, 172)

Creation is essentially revelatory. Humanity's uncoerced acceptance of responsibility for its custody places human beings squarely as collaborators in divine revelation to the extent that they are theoretically capable of obliterating God's signs from one another's sight. I say "theoretically," for, given an outright confrontation, God's sovereignty always takes precedence over human freedom. Humankind's ways of dealing with created nature directly reflect attitudes toward the Creator.[7]

Islam and Economics

As the Qur'an's reference to "striving with your possessions" (or wealth) suggests, Islamic tradition considers economic affairs part of the comprehensive notion of jihad. The search for economic justice and equity is a crucial aspect of striving in the way of God. Numerous verses of the Qur'an and even more numerous Hadiths address mercantile and fiscal concerns, from weights and measures to inheritance to compensation for services rendered. In the second half of the twentieth century Muslim writers have shown increasing interest in formulating the principles of an explicitly Islamic theory. Scholars in a variety of contexts across the world have addressed the matter. One situation in which the need for an Islamic economics has been most keenly perceived has been that of revolutionary Iran. Chapter 3 will describe in greater detail how the two main segments of the greater Islamic community, the Sunni and the Shi'i, differ from each other. Here we shall focus on several attempts to interpret the duty to "strive with one's possessions" in the context of the Islamic Republic of Iran. Iranian Shi'ism receives special attention here and in the next chapter because, although Shi'i Muslims comprise only about ten percent of the total Muslim population, recent events have raised much curiosity among non-Muslims about the nature of the Iranian experiment in promoting an Islamic Republic.

One of the leading figures during the Khumayni era was Ayatullah Mahmud Taleghani (1911–1979). During one of his many prison terms under the second Pahlavi Shah, Taleghani completed a book on the philosophy of property called *Islam and Ownership* (in Comparison to the Economic Systems of the West). Taleghani's ideological point of departure is the prophetic paradigm of Madina as ideal society.

> In this model city [Madina in Muhammad's time] . . . wealth was divided equally and according to need among all the people. There was no distinction between individuals, and no distinction between the governor and the governed except in matter of state administration. There was no visible difference between them in attire or housing. Everyone considered himself a responsible participant in public affairs, and . . . this superb model of collective effort and sharing was largely preserved until the time of the caliphs (mid-seventh century]. Later on, the Islamic world took on a capitalist hue, and it deviated from the principles of that initial model.[8]

For Taleghani as for so many Muslim authors, Muhammad's Madina symbolizes the golden age in every respect, the perfect implementation of Islam's "essence." His book is less a treatise on the science of economics than an attempt to reflect on how Islamic values can be used to interpret a broad range of societal issues with economic implications. Eight chapters deal with the evolution of the concept of ownership, the emergence of labor as a force, a critique of Marxism, a view of economy from the perspective of Islamic faith, the foundation of Islamic economics and the origins of its regulations, problems caused by the use of money, fourteen distinctive characteristics of Islamic economics, and the origins of social stratification.

At the heart of Taleghani's approach is a notion of justice: justice is not merely "whatever God happens to do," but something God virtually must do. Intellectually in sympathy with the Mu'tazila of old (emphasizing that God must act according to the canons of Reason), this is anything but the resigned fatalism non-Muslims so often associate with Islamic thought. According to the concept of justice suggested in Taleghani and other recent Iranian authors, one is not obliged to acquiesce in the rule of a tyrant who is known to be unjust, hoping in the meanwhile that God's justice will become evident in the eschaton. Here the emphasis is on human responsibility: "As Islam attests to the reality of human potentials and talents, it considers man, with his special composition, as the founder of society, economy, and history."[9]

If human participation in securing justice is the heart of the matter, acknowledgment of God's unity (*tawhid*), and therefore repudiation of all forms of idolatry (*shirk*, setting up "partners" with God) is the soul. Divine sovereignty is the theological foundation for Shi'i theories of property and ownership, which in turn provided a thematic justification for the overthrow of the shah. Tawhid is the ultimate hedge against tyranny (*taghut*, transgressing, hybris, overflowing the boundaries of one's humanity). With divine lordship as the starting point, the argument goes:

> Ownership is relative and limited. Ownership means the authority and power of possession. As human power and authority are limited, no person should consider himself the absolute power and complete possessor. Absolute power and complete possession belong only to God. . . . Man's ownership then is limited to what ever God has wisely willed and to the capacity of his intellect, authority, and freedom granted to him.[10]

In this as in other regards, Shi'i theorists like Taleghani seek to set Islamic economics apart from capitalism (free and unlimited ownership) and collectivism (negation of private property), both of which are seen to permit or even necessitate tyranny or dictatorship.

One can hardly describe adequately in a few paragraphs the kind of fascinating thinking one finds in Taleghani and, for example, in the *Economics of Tawhid* by former Iranian president Abulhasan Bani Sadr. For now, however, a summary of some of the specific issues to which the Shi'i theorists are attempting to respond in a general way may help to concretize the context of their search for an Islamic economics.

Economic tyranny means specifically over a century and a half of foreign influence in Iranian affairs. The Treaty of Turkomanchai of 1828, which ended Iran's war with Russia, exempted foreign traders from the internal tariffs paid by Iranian merchants. Increasing royal interest in foreign travel and goods meant higher taxes for the peasantry, with tax collectors keeping far more than they handed in. Iran's first roads were built in the late nineteenth century by the British and Russians, but for their own use. In 1890 the shah granted a tobacco monopoly to a British merchant, sparking off a movement in 1891–1892 that was modern Iran's first successful coordinated anti-government protest, involving many segments of society.

Throughout the nineteenth century, private land ownership grew. Increasing demand for the export of such cash crops as cotton and opium by landlords led to increasing social stratification, greater wealth for landlords and bigger merchants, less income for the peasantry, and shortages of food crops with the price of wheat at home soaring because of rises in wheat exports.[11] With the twentieth century came foreign oil concessions and what many considered deplorable Iranian dependence on outside money. Worse still, need for American loans has been seen as the reason for the Iranian parliament's granting all Americans in Iran legal immunity, prior to 1979, with respect to crimes they might commit there.[12]

Among the shah's economic policies, it was perhaps his

program of land reform that became the single most frequent target of revolutionary critics. A showpiece of the "White Revolution" became a rallying point for the Islamic revolution. The four stage program begun in 1962 attempted to centralize by weakening the independent landlords, incorporating peasant property, reducing Iran's economic dependence on agriculture and thus on a labor-intensive source, and shifting to oil as a source more readily controllable by the central government.[13] Khumayni's evaluation of the program: the shah's claim that he would make the peasants independent cultivators has destroyed the agararian economy entirely, left Iran dependent on imported essentials, and simply created another market for American—and worse still, Israeli—goods.[14]

What the search for an Islamic economics has produced thus far is the articulation of a global ideology aimed at forming a new economy and society. It does not analyze an existing reality on economic terms, but seeks to replace a corrupt order with a moral one. Islamic economics is, as economist Homa Katouzian sees it, idealistic and romantic in that it underemphasizes major problems; pragmatic to the extent that it skirts doctrinal difficulties by means of ad hoc and sometimes arbitrary interpretations of questions that Islamic law does not pronounce clearly either required or forbidden; and universalistic in that it wants to internationalize land and natural resources, but fails to deal with any specifics of international economic relations.[15]

In particular, though revolutionary figures do agree on such socio-economic values as redistribution of money, renewal of agriculture, cessation of wasteful projects, and more suitable uses of technology, Shi'i economics does not adequately address certain specific issues, as anthropologist Michael Fischer indicates. First, it provides no specific mechanism with which to oversee the interplay between common good and individual rights in matters of ownership as well as general economic relations. Second, the idea that anyone is allowed to appropriate whatever resources he can use seems to presuppose both abundant resources and small scale organization. The theory of ownership is not adequate to an industrialized society. Third, theorists simply assume that the traditional Qur'anic injuctions concerning taxation will work in a complex industrial society. And finally, the Qur'an prohibits the earning through loans of what is called *riba,* but theorists have not been able to agree on whether that involves the prohibition of all interest, or merely of unjust interest (usury). Clearly there can be no stable banking system until such a key issue can be worked out.[16] All in all, since Muslims regard their tradition as constituting a comprehensive scheme for an integral world, one can expect to see increasing attention to the challenge of forging an Islamic economics in years to come. The late eminent Muslim economist Khurshid Ahmad sums up his theory of economics and development this way:

> Islam stands for effort (i.e. striving), struggle, movement and reconstruction—elements of social change. It is not merely a set of beliefs. It also provides a definite outlook on life and a programme for action . . . a comprehensive milieu for social reconstruction.

He proceeds to enumerate several "basic propositions about the dynamics of social change as they reveal themselves by reflection on the Qur'an and Sunna." He begins by ruling out historical determinism; humankind therefore has to take the initiative for change. Of all forces, human effort is the most efficacious in changing the world. That change must be not only environmental, but within each person's heart. And finally, since change involves the disruption of many basic relationships, it is the responsibility of the Muslim to see that all sweeping change occurs gradually and as a balanced evolution. In this respect, he sees the essential Islamic value to be "innovation coupled with integration."[17]

Islam and Human Rights

Closely related to the Islamic concern for economic justice is the desire not to let the rights of the individual become swallowed up by those of society as a whole. It seeks a balance between the rampant individualism many Muslims associate with capitalist cultures, and the stifling of individual initiative frequently identified with totalitarian systems. Muslims think of Islam as the last bastion of genuine egalitarianism under God. Like all the rest of us, they have had a hard time translating ideals into realities. Here again our concern is not to review or critique any performance record, but to sum up the ideals Islamic tradition has proposed. In any case, to the degree that Muslims have been party to infringement on human rights or the perpetration of unjustifiable hostilities, it may be helpful to recall that what G.K. Chesterton said of Christianity is equally applicable to Islam. It is not so much that it has failed as that it has never really been tried.

Muslims trace the origin of "human rights" issues in their tradition back to Muhammad. Two early documents form the basic charter. Shortly after the Hijra, Muhammad promulgated what came to be known as the "Constitution of Madina," in which he set out the principal terms governing the relationships of Muslims to one another and to the non-Muslim groups in the region.[18] Equally fundamental are several of the stipulations of Muhammad's "Farewell Sermon," delivered in 632 C.E. during his final pilgrimage to Makka. In the document one finds basic statements concerning crucial

Shir Dar (Lion-bearer) Madrasa (1616–36), in Samarkand, Uzbekistan, showing elaborate tile decoration characteristic of Persian and Central Asian Islamic architectural styles.

social relationships. One can get a sense of its tone from this sample:

> Your lives and property are sacred and inviolable among one another. . . . [You] have rights over your wives and your wives have rights over you. Treat your wives with kindness and love. . . . The aristocracy of yore is trampled under my feet. The Arab has no superiority over the non-Arab and the non-Arab has no superiority over the Arab. All are children of Adam and Adam was made of earth. . . . Know that all Muslims are brothers unto one another. Ye are one brotherhood. Nothing which belongs to another is lawful unto his brother, unless freely given out of goodwill. Guard yourselves against committing injustice. . . .[19]

Concerned Muslims in our time have focused considerable attention on questions of human rights. As is the case with human rights organizations all over the world, those that have formed within the greater Islamic community often have lacked the political clout needed to bring about effective change in governmental policy. Evidence of violations, apparently sanctioned at the highest levels in certain nations whose populations are predominantly Muslim, has prompted some outside observers to criticize Muslims for failing to safeguard basic human rights. The charge is misdirected. Critics would argue that where Muslims are "in control," and preach the unity of religious and civil spheres, they have no excuse for not implementing Islam's loftiest values in their societies. Such criticism might be right on the mark but for a pair of unpleasant realities. First, when ostensibly religious ideals are explicitly incorporated into political programs they often get pushed aside by more pressing pragmatic concerns, even as government spokespersons continue to employ religious rhetoric. Second, religious ideals that are so appropriated are often quite selective, do not represent the tradition's full scope, and thus fail to take account of conflicting claims.

Islamic ideals in this respect are extremely high and, like all such challenging aspirations, very difficult to put into practice. One can cite numerous examples of Muslim efforts to articulate in contemporary terms the principles of human rights. About ten years ago, Pakistan hosted an International Islamic Seminar on the Application of the Revealed Law. In a statement obviously meant to refute a number of charges, the Seminar declared: " . . . the Islamic code of life lays down not only moral, but social, economic, political, cultural and educational norms and rules based on the principles of equality, brotherhood and justice . . . the Islamic code is designed to create a just and free society in which every individual enjoys equal rights and equal opportunities regardless of rank, birth, caste, colour, or creed."[20]

Muslim writers often situate human rights within the context of "God's Rights." God has the right to, but no need of, human beings' faith, acceptance of divine guidance, obedience and worship. Here obviously there is room for serious misunderstanding between Muslims and non-Muslims. In the verse immediately after the Throne Verse we find the very direct statement, "There is no compulsion in religion." (Qur'an 2:256) Many Muslims take that to mean that all persons are free to respond to God's signs as they please. Islamic history is full of examples of what Marshal Hodgson calls the triumph of the universalistic spirit, in which Muslims and non-Muslims lived together in harmony. At times, however, the spirit of "communalism" has dominated, with disastrous consequences.[21] To the matter of inter-religious relations we shall return shortly.

A "Universal Islamic Declaration of Human Rights" promulgated by the Islamic Council in 1981 represents the fullest modern day articulation of Islamic values on the subject. The document affirms a "commitment to uphold the following inviolable and inalienable human rights that we consider are enjoined by Islam"—right to life, freedom, equality, justice, fair trial, protection vs. abuse of power or torture, protection of reputation, asylum, minority protection, participation in public affairs, freedom of belief, thought and speech, freedom of religion, free association, economic order, protection of property, worker dignity, social security, family integrity, protection of rights of married women, education, privacy, freedom of movement and residence.[22]

An area of Islamic human rights that non-Muslims have often cited in recent times as problematical is the place of women in society. Outsiders frequently fault Islam for failing to secure the kind of social equality that would allow women to pursue careers outside the home. As a prime example, some critics point to the recent arrest of a number of Saudi women who violated a ban on driving automobiles. But if "Islam" is the operative value system in this instance, one must ask why in so many other predominantly Muslim countries all over the world most women do not wear veils and are free to drive cars. And in neighboring Jordan, the government has recently hired over sixty women to serve as mosque preachers, while numerous other women now study in Shari'a schools once open only to men. Actual practices in relation to these and other similar social issues are clearly too complex and variegated to be explained by reference to Islamic religious injunctions.

One has to keep a number of factors in mind when presuming to sit in judgment of other cultural and religious systems. First, no humanly devised social structure is perfectly just, and that includes those that claim divine sanction. Second, all cultures and societies have their unchallenged assumptions, and are subject to a certain amount of upheaval when someone chooses to challenge those assumptions. Third, one cannot simply impose one's own preferences on another culture; cultural differences come about as close to an absolute value as anything in human experience. One cannot simply transplant into other cultural settings everything that Americans think essential to individual freedom. Finally, though there may be a fine line between certain unquestioned practices in a given society, and violations of human rights, outside observers have the duty to look for that line and not simply assume that those under scrutiny have crossed it.[23]

Islam and International Relations: War and Peace

Many non-Muslims express misgivings about many of what they take to be Islamic values. They are often frankly afraid because they have formed an impression of Islam as a warlike religious tradition. Many people have unfortunately and most unfairly come to expect that behind every episode of hostage-taking or large-scale terrorism there lurks a band of swarthy, bloodthirsty Arab or Iranian Muslims. Every time journalists use the term "jihad," either as part of some faction's name, or to describe the "holy war" some leader has allegedly called for, millions of listeners or readers have their worst fears confirmed. "There they go again!" one hears people say too often, citing such examples as Khumayni's death sentence on Salman Rushdie and Saddam Husayn's attempts to galvanize Islamic support for a Jihad against all infidels defiling sacred Arabian soil.

Questions abound concerning the sanctioning of violent means, which Islamic tradition shares with more than one other major religious tradition. There is no doubt that it is an important issue about which we need to understand several complex aspects. First, Muslims regard Muhammad as model; second, we need to appreciate the actual aspirations of many millions of Muslims for a life of peace; third, conditions governing authentic Jihad are numerous and demanding; and finally, we Americans and Europeans must endeavor to appreciate the depth of feeling that the foreign policy of powers dominating world affairs over the past century has engendered in populations across the globe, and especially in the Middle East. We shall look at each of these in turn.

Muhammad again stands out as the prime exemplar of the ideal mode of fostering peaceful relations among interest groups and communities that are defined by overlapping or otherwise conflicting claims. The story of the Prophet's replacing the Black Stone in the Ka'ba suggests, along with other traditional accounts, that Muhammad developed a public reputation very early as a trustworthy person endowed with very effective negotiating skills. When envoys came south from Yathrib (later Madina) to offer Muhammad and the Muslim community a new home, part of what they wanted in return was that Muhammad act as arbitrator in various factional disputes then besetting the citizens of Yathrib.

Tradition cites prominently Muhammad's diplomacy in forging treaties and alliances. It emphasizes especially Muhammad's preference for peaceful means and the centrality Muhammad accorded to the reconciliation of hearts. Still it is exceedingly difficult to penetrate the veil of dark images that has over the centuries shrouded the picture of Muhammad that dominated the thinking of so many non-Muslims. When non-Muslims read, for example, of Muhammad's decision to resort to military action against the Jewish tribes of Madina, they are shocked. They may even find their attention so riveted on those truly unhappy events that they are unable to see anything positive in the early history of the Muslim community. At the opposite end of the spectrum, Muhammad remains for Muslims the paragon of gentleness and concern for the needs of people. One always needs to look for the truth somewhere in between the ideal of utter perfection most communities see in their foundational figures, and the jaundiced view taken by people who for a wide range of reasons prefer to cling to predominantly negative interpretations.

The vast majority of Muslims long for a world at peace. They sincerely believe that Islamic values seek to promote the possibility of such a world. Their tradition, they believe, stands not only for the absence of war, but that positive state of safety and security and freedom from anxiety that uniquely results from the condition of grateful surrender to God in faith (*islam, iman*). Those of us who get our entire picture of Muslims from media coverage of current events need to understand that we suffer from tunnel vision. Any Malaysian or Pakistani television viewer who relied on that medium to convey a sense of American values might very well develop a similarly truncated picture of Americans. How many American soldiers camped on Saudi sand could be heard to express not only willingness but positive eagerness to fight?

Islamic criteria governing the call for a Jihad against an outward enemy are as stringent as Christianity's terms for waging a "just war." Moreover, Muslim specialists differ as widely as do Christian theologians as to the circumstances under which one can claim to have met those criteria. In addition, one must distinguish between popular sentiment and the core of a faith tradition. Most Muslims are as unfamiliar with the classic conditions for Jihad as their Christian counterparts are with their tradition's criteria for a "just war." For example, no action can be justified as authentic Jihad if any of the following conditions obtain: killing non-combatants, prisoners of war or diplomatic personnel; use of poisonous weapons (beginning with poison-tipped arrows and swords, for example) or inhumane means to kill; atrocities in conquered lands, including mutilation of persons and animals, and wanton despoilation of natural resources; and the sexual abuse of captive women.

Islamic tradition dating from the earliest military encounters between the Muslims of Madina and other groups includes numerous guidelines on these and other such issues. Legislation of peacetime relations likewise lays down specific obligations in the conduct of international trade, the use of slaves, the conclusion of treaties, diplomatic protection, recognition of sovereignty, and the right to asylum. All of that, however, has not prevented horrors from being perpetrated in the very name of Islam, to the great sorrow of many millions of Muslims. Nothing can excuse those who engage in such atrocities, whatever their express motivation, whatever their avowed religious affiliation.

In many instances what we outsiders see Muslims doing in other parts of the world is not so very different from what we would do in an instant if we were in their shoes. The Afghan rebels have called their struggle against Russian military occupation a Jihad, identifying themselves as *mujahidin.* Indeed the law of Jihad does allow for military response to an invasion of one's territorial sovereignty. Numerous groups of Muslims who use the word Jihad in their names genuinely believe that their actions are justifiable and done precisely in defense, for they perceive foreign presence in their part of the world as invasive and unwelcome. What is most important to note here is this: on balance, Islamic tradition simply does not encourage, let alone recommend unreservedly, violent solutions to human problems.[24]

Islam and Interreligious Relations

Several Qur'anic texts speak of God's plan in creating the world in all its human diversity. "O humankind! We created you male and female, and we made you into peoples and tribes that you might learn to know one another. Indeed God considers the noblest among you those of most reverent awe [of God]." (Qur'an 49:13; see also 30:22, 14:4) More specifically, several texts speak of diversity in the context of plural communities of faith. God could have made humankind all of one group, but instead left the human race composed of many segments in order to test and challenge human beings to work things out with each other. Frequent references to "vying with one another in good deeds" set the tone of all human, and especially religious, relationships. "We have made for each among you a revealed road (*shir'a,* related to term shari'a) and a way to travel. Had God wished, he would have made you a single community, but [God wished] to test you according to what he has given each of you. Therefore vie with one another in good deeds, for God is the final goal for all of you, and it is he who will clarify for you those things about which you now argue." (Qur'an 5:48; see also 2:148 and 23:61)

Beginning with the Qur'an, Islamic tradition possesses a well articulated attitude toward other faith communities. No other world religious scripture of the Qur'an's antiquity contains such a clearly articulated approach to this matter. It employs three terms to denote the several dimensions of human religious life. First, *din* refers to religiousness in the most general form. As a fundamental impulse that God infuses into every person, *din* has always been one and the same. It implies the basic attitude of grateful surrender in a generic sense. That original unity of human religious response ramified into different groups for a variety of reasons (see e.g. Qur'an 2:213, 23:51–4). Even though God sent a new messenger to correct the deviations that occurred through history, many people chose not to accept the corrective and kept to the old ways.

Second, the Qur'an uses the term *milla* to refer to specific religious traditions that arose as a result, such as that of Abraham for example. A third term, *umma,* refers to a second dimension of religious diversity, what one Muslim writer calls "religio-moral and socio-political community." God has allowed humankind to become religiously diverse precisely as a test and an impetus to a beneficial moral competition.[25]

According to the Qur'an, Muslims have a special relationship to certain other religious communities. Especially in post-Hijra texts, the Qur'an speaks of Muslims as having much in common with the "Peoples of the Book." The term originally referred to Jews and Christians, and eventually expanded to include other communities as well. These groups were known as *dhimmis* or protected communities. And the notion that "there is no compulsion in religious matters" (*din,* Qur'an 2:256) is surely a central concept in Islamic views of relations with other traditions. But there is no doubt that the ultimate goal is a return to the pristine unity in which all creation worships God together. There is also no doubt that non-Muslims living in largely Muslim nations have sometimes confronted odious restrictions in religious practice. The realities of inter-religious relations have not always been cordial, and much difficult work needs to be done on this matter all over the world. When it comes to acceptance of diversity, all human beings have a hard time moving from theory to practice.

We close this chapter with a classic story about Abraham that captures something of both problems and prospects in this arena. According to an oft retold tradition, Abraham was in the habit of postponing his breakfast each day until some hungry wayfarer should happen by his house. Abraham would then invite the stranger in to share his table. One day an old man came along. As he and Abraham were about to refresh themselves, Abraham began to pronounce a blessing.

When he noted that the old man's lips formed the words of another prayer, that of a Zoroastrian, Abraham became incensed and drove the stranger away. God was not pleased. He reprimanded Abraham, saying, "I have given this man life and food for a hundred years. Could you not give him hospitality for one day, even if he does homage to fire?" Abraham immediately went after the old man and brought him back home. Abraham, already known as the paragon of hospitality, thus becomes also the model of openness to religious diversity. Even to the "Friend of the Merciful" (*Khalil ar-Rahman*) that virtue apparently did not come naturally.

Questions for Discussion

1. How many different ways can one interpret the significance of Hijra for Muslims? Compare Hijra in its various meanings with the biblical Jewish experience of Exodus. Do any other religious traditions speak of similar notions? Can one find evidence of Hijra-like experiences in the lives of foundational figures other than Muhammad, such as Abraham, Jesus, Buddha, or perhaps even Lao-Tze?

2. What kind of personal meaning might the Hijra have for an individual Muslim? How might it serve as a guiding or formative concept in an individual's personal growth?

3. What is the fundamental meaning of the concept of Jihad? How many different variations on that basic meaning has Islamic tradition developed? Can you find similar concepts at the heart of other religious traditions? Why do you think non-Muslims so often unfairly associate Islam with violence?

4. What are some fundamental Islamic religious responses to the perception of "signs on the horizons"? Are there paral-

lels in the religious practices of other major traditions? How do "natural symbols" function in Islamic ritual? In that of other traditions?

5. How do Islamic values impinge on such global issues as economics, environment, international relations, human rights, and relationships among the major religious traditions? How does the example of Muhammad touch on these matters?

3

Hajj: Signs Among Believers and Return to the Center on the Main Road (Shari'a)

One of the richest aspects of religious thought and practice is that of pilgrimage. No community of faith has developed a stronger sense of pilgrimage's literal and symbolic centrality than has Islam. Just as Hijra has become a powerful metaphor for Muslims' understanding of their place within the world and the larger human community, so Hajj epitomizes their sense of identity as a unique community of faith. Striving to avoid all extremes, Islam has thought of itself as both a "middle community" and an unswervingly centered community. "We have therefore fashioned you into an Umma in equilibrium so that you might be witness to humankind and that the Messenger [Muhammad] might be a witness to you." (Qur'an 2:143)

As a prophetic paradigm, pilgrimage has roots in Abraham's legendary sojourn in Makka and his building (or rebuilding in versions in which Adam built the original) of the Ka'ba with the help of his son Isma'il. More immediately, the Prophet Muhammad legitimized the practice by combining various elements of pre-Islamic ritual and proclaiming the whole complex Islamic. Perhaps more than any other fundamental of Islamic tradition, pilgrimage symbolizes the community and equality of persons before God, and embodies the intense longing many Muslims feel for a humanity healed of its divisions.

Indian calendar poster depicting emblems of the two
principal Islamic sacred sites: the black-draped Ka'ba
in Makka on the left, and the green-domed tomb of the
Prophet in Madina on the right. Rays of light emanate from
the symbolic number 786 above, derived from the numerical
value of the Arabic letters in the phrase "In the name of
God." The rose below is sometimes used as a symbolic
allusion to Muhammad. Photo courtesy of Carl Ernst.

In this chapter we examine the role of pilgrimage as prophetic exemplar, as practice and as metaphor for community. We shall discuss several dimensions of the idea. First pilgrimage's historical connections and development within the history of Islamic spirituality provide necessary background. Second, the concept of "signs among believers," paralleling "signs on the horizons" and "signs within the self," has been based in the Qur'an's "verse-signs" and elaborated in the central Islamic religious institutions of law, its models of leadership and of religious authority. And third, we find that Muslims have always responded to those signs in a wide range of ways.

Hajj as Metaphor for Return to the Center

Since long before Muhammad's time, Makka had been a center of pilgrimage. In his younger days Muhammad had prayed at the Ka'ba in the heart of the city, along with countless other people from all over the Arabian peninsula. The Ka'ba in his time was a simple, nearly cubic shaped structure of dark stone. In one of its four corners was set a black stone, an ovoid somewhat larger than a bowling ball, now fractured into seven pieces and framed in a collar of silver.

Such stones had long been part of local religious centers in the Arabian peninsula, and throughout the greater Middle East. In the Hebrew scripture, stone pillars had been both signs of contention, when they were at the center of idolatrous cults, and altogether acceptable symbols of help and witness. When Joshua, for example, gathered the people of Israel together to renew their special relationship with God, he set up a stone and called upon it to witness in its mute integrity how the people had reaffirmed the covenant (Jos 24). Popular tradition has it that the Ka'ba's black stone has likewise been taking note of momentous events—the rise and fall of the power-ful, the making and breaking of oaths—since the very dawn of creation. At the appropriate moment, it will reveal all.

The Ka'ba and its stone had many meanings to the Makkans of Muhammad's day, and they played an important role, sometimes negative and sometimes more positive, in the Prophet's life. According to one account, when the structure had to be rebuilt, the Makkans asked Muhammad the Trust-worthy to replace the stone in its socket. Ever aware of the symbolic value of his public actions, and looking for ways to unify local factions, Muhammad placed the stone in the cen-ter of his cloak and had representatives of the chief interests lift it with him by grabbing a corner of the cloak. Some esti-mates date that event at around the year 604 C.E., prior to the beginning of Muhammad's prophetic career. As the Quraysh came more and more to disapprove of his new preaching, they applied the ultimate social pressure, denying Muham-mad access to the sacred precincts to pray.

In the year 630 C.E. the Muslims came down from Ma-dina to claim Makka for Islam. One of the Prophet's first acts was to cleanse the Ka'ba of its idols, traditionally said to have numbered three hundred and sixty, one for each day of the lunar year. Since then the "cube" (one of the variations on the root *Ka'aBa* means "to dice into cubes") has remained empty except for a number of hanging lamps. Each year the Saudis perform a ritual reenactment of Muhammad's initial purifica-tion. When Muhammad returned to Makka to make his "fare-well pilgrimage" in 632 C.E., he sanctified definitively the Ka'ba and the sites in the vicinity of Makka, making them forever integral to the Muslim ritual of the Hajj or "greater pilgrimage."

All aspects of the sanctuary and its environs are bathed in an aura of prophetic sanctity and antiquity. There are, of course, many unanswered questions as to the historicity of the events that tradition associates with this spiritual center. But let us imagine for a moment that we could look at this revered place through the eyes of ancient Islamic tradition. Were Abraham to return to Makka now, he would surely be surprised at how the sacred precincts have changed since the early days. The Ka'ba has been rebuilt several times and is now probably quite a bit larger than in Muhammad's time, standing now some forty-three feet high—about three times its sixth century height, with its four sides ranging in width from about thirty-six to forty-three feet. The most recent major renovations occurred in the mid 1950s when the Saudi royal family enlarged the existing sixteenth century Ottoman Turkish structure designed by Sinan, Sulayman the Magnificent's chief architect. Before the door, which is now elevated seven feet above ground level, Abraham would note that the spot where he once stood to pray is marked by a small copper-gold cupola that encloses the stone that became waxen under his feet.

Over the place where his wife Hagar is said to have run to and fro in frantic search for water to give her thirsty baby Isma'il, Abraham would find a massive covered path connecting the two small hills Safa and Marwa. He would see there pilgrims reenacting Hagar's moment of panic, and from there repairing to a spot near the Ka'ba, just below present ground level, to sip the water of Zamzam that miraculously bubbled up where the baby had pummeled the sand with his feet. Outside Makka, in the plain of Arafat, Abraham would revisit other memorable sites: where Satan had tempted him to disobey God, where he had prepared to sacrifice his only son—Isma'il, according to most Islamic sources—and where Muslims now ritually offer up sheep or camels to recall how God supplied Abraham's sacrificial animal.

In addition to the rituals that specifically recall the deeds of the prophet Abraham and his family, the Hajj proper includes also the remembrance of Muhammad's paradigmatic pilgrimage and his farewell sermon outside of Makka in the valley of Arafat. The formal season of Hajj extends from the eighth to the thirteenth of the last lunar month. When pilgrims come to Makka outside of that period, they may make the "lesser pilgrimage" or *'umra,* which involves chiefly the rituals associated with the sanctuary of the Ka'ba—donning the white pilgrim's garb, called *ihram;* circumambulation; and the running between Safa and Marwa.

Not part of the Hajj strictly speaking are several commemorative actions associated with Muhammad that most Muslims strive to perform while on Hajj. Most significant is the visit to the Prophet's mosque in Madina, where a green dome now covers what was once his house and where Muhammad is buried along with his daughter Fatima and his father-in-law and successor as first Caliph, Abu Bakr.

Just as Hijra has come to mean something more than an historic event that occurred fourteen centuries ago, so Hajj manifests several levels of meaning in Islamic spirituality. All Muslims are enjoined to make Hajj if they can; but in practice, only a small percentage of the world's Muslims enjoy the privilege of doing so in the flesh. This has been so since the earliest days of Islam. The hope remains high, however, for countless thousands who will never actually make the journey; and all who wish for it can make pilgrimage in spirit. As with all other Islamic ritual observances, the ultimate significance lies in their power to manifest inward transformation and conviction. A certain kind of pilgrimage narrative has become practically a genre unto itself. Stories tell of people ready to sacrifice everything, including their families and their own lives, to make pilgrimage, and end up with the moral that staying home and taking care of one's primary responsibilities more than satisfies as one's Hajj.[1] Classical sources have often described the desire for pilgrimage as a longing to stand where earth meets heaven, a desire to meet God. Sometimes even a definitive encounter with a spiritual master or guide is said to fulfill the requirements of pilgrimage. However one describes the essential Hajj, imagery of the Ka'ba figures prominently. Let us look at how that imagery has informed Islamic spirituality.

The Ka'ba represents journey's end, first of all, because it is the symbolic point of origin of all creation. Around it all things turn; from it all things radiate. What the human heart is to the microcosm, the Ka'ba is to the macrocosm, namely, the focus of desire to return to the source. Poets have often spoken of the Ka'ba of faith or hope or love, or of whatever virtue, power or quality one regards as most needed or sought after at any given moment.

Some poets consider Muhammad himself as the Ka'ba of prophetic revelation, and the Black Stone as the Seal of his Prophethood, the sign of his definitive mission. Jalal ad-Din Rumi, of whom we have spoken briefly earlier, calls the physical Ka'ba an extension of the Ka'ba of the heart. He develops the association between Prophet and Ka'ba in his story of how it is possible to regard a certain spiritual guide as the Ka'ba. In that story, the famous mystic Bayazid al-Bistami (d. 874) was on his way to Makka when he encountered a shaykh. When Bayazid told the shaykh of his destination, the shaykh told him he would do as well circumambulating *him* seven times. Bayazid could realize the blessings of Pilgrimage, and many times more, merely by laying his pilgrimage bankroll at the shaykh's feet. In the shaykh's words:

> The Ka'ba is indeed the House of His worship; but this form of mine in which He created me also contains knowledge of Him.
>
> Since God built the Ka'ba, never once has He entered into it; but into this house of my body, none but God has ever gone.

To have seen me is to have seen God. You have
walked around the Ka'ba of Sincerity.
To have served me is to have obeyed and given glory
to God. Never think of God as separate from me.
Open your eyes and take a good look at me; you may
thus see the Light of God in a human being.

The story takes the shaykh to be a "type" of the Prophet, for
he paraphrases the Hadith, "Who has seen me has seen God,"
and recalls the Qur'an's teaching that to obey the Messenger
is to obey God. What Rumi is suggesting here is that a pilgrimage made ostensibly to the House (i.e. Muhammad or
the spiritual guide) is in reality a journey to the Lord of the
House. The process of enlisting the aid of a spiritual guide
(*shaykh* in Arabic, *pir* in Persian) therefore both models and is
modeled on the Pilgrimage.[2]

Sharafuddin Maneri, a fourteenth century Indian spiritual leader, tells another story about Bayazid. In this case the
traveler comes to Makka not once, but three times, acquiring
with each arrival a deeper knowledge of the Goal. Bayazid
tells his story:

When I went to the Holy Place and saw the beauty of the
Kaaba, I said to myself: "I have seen much better materials than those employed in the construction of this building!" I desired the Lord of the House. I returned home.
The following year when I reached the Holy Place, I
opened the eyes of my conscience and saw not only the
house but the Lord of the House. I said: "In the divine
world there is no room for anything except God, in the
world of the Divine Unity duality is excluded. The Beloved, the house, and I would be three: Anyone who perceived duality would be an unbeliever, and yet I see three:
How can I avoid being a heretic?" I returned home. The
third year, when I reached the Holy Place, the divine

favor swept me into its embrace; the curtain of whatever
is not God was removed from my power of discernment;
my heart was illumined with the flame of mystical knowledge; my being was inflamed with the lights of divine
illumination; and this saying filled my head: "You have
come to visit Me with an honest heart, and the One who is
visited has the right to bless the one who visits Him."[3]

Pursuing the Qur'anic theme mentioned above, that true
piety is essentially linked not to facing East or West but to
belief in God and the Judgment Day (Qur'an 2:177), the
thirteenth century Egyptian mystic Ibn al-Farid (d. 1235) addressed an ode to the Divine Presence as the Ka'ba of Perfect Beauty.

O Ka'ba of Splendor, toward your beauty the hearts of
those intent on you make pilgrimage and cry, "Twice at
your pleasure!" [A ritual phrase often repeated by pilgrims.] Lightning blazing through mountain passes has
brought us the finest of gifts: your flashing smile, reveal-
ing to my eye that my heart was your neighbor; and I
longed for the full vision of your loveliness. But for you
I would not have sought guidance in lightning, and my
heart would not have saddened and wept at birdsong
from forest depths. Still, the lightning guided me, and
birds on their branches of wood sang me past need of
tunes from lute of wood. For so long I have wanted you to
look my way, and how much blood have I shed between
desire and fulfillment! They called me fearless before
I came to love you; but I have set bravery aside and no
longer hold myself in safety. My endurance has fled from
me and I am led captive; my former sadness gone, new
grief has come to my aid. Will you not turn from your
aversion, from your preference for tyranny over kind-
ness, from cruelty will you not turn? Greatest of all gifts
would be your slaking the thirst of one at the point of

death, that he might revive. It is not my longing for one
beside you that has wasted me: out of affection for you
alone have I perished. The beauty of your face has quick-
ened me and left me dead, for I am barred even from
kissing its veil.[4]

Everyone who journeys toward God's splendor is on Pilgrimage. God's smile flashes as lightning through mountain
passes en route, enticing the wayfarer to yearn for the full
vision of God. What else could lure someone out of a safe
haven onto a perilous road? the poet wonders. The last line
here alludes to the veil or *kiswa* over the Ka'ba; as the poet
continues, he laments the loss of his youth and friends. His
longing for the Ka'ba has made chaos of his life. At length
God rewards Ibn al-Farid's long-suffering, lifting the veil
from the Ka'ba and showing the seeker his Face. We shall
return to some of the poet's themes in the context of the
individual's perception of God's signs in Chapter 4.

According to noted anthropologists Victor and Edith
Turner, pilgrimage is "extroverted mysticism, just as mysticism is introverted pilgrimage. . . . The pilgrim physically
traverses a mystical way; the mystic sets forth on an interior
pilgrimage."[5] A marvelous tale by the Persian poet Farid ad-
Din Attar (d. 1220), entitled *The Conference of the Birds,* admirably illustrates the concept of mystical pilgrimage.

Once upon a time, all the birds of the world assembled
to discuss their place in creation. They decided that they, no
less than the other animal kingdoms, ought to have a king. In
their quest for the feathered monarch, however, they would
need an experienced guide. Fortunately one of their number,
the crested Hoopoe, had served the prophet Solomon as his
ambassador to the Queen of Sheba. The Hoopoe volunteered
his services. In his inaugural address he announced that the
birds indeed already had a king who dwelt in a mysterious

and mountainous land many days distant. Experienced in the demands of life in the Unseen World, the Hoopoe warned that the journey would be arduous.

One after another the birds stood up to express their misgivings and offer excuses for staying at home. To each in turn the Hoopoe responded with a further elaboration of the importance of the journey and the magnificent prospect of meeting the King, the Simurgh. We are but the King's shadow on earth, he went on; and though none of us is truly fit to gaze on the King's beauty directly, "by his abounding grace he has given us a mirror to reflect himself, and this mirror is the heart. Look into your heart and there you will see his image."

Seven perilous valleys must the birds traverse. Quest, Love, Understanding, Detachment, acknowledgement of God's Unity, Bewilderment, and, at last, Poverty and Death to Self lay before all willing to go forth. By the end survivors numbered only thirty birds (*si*=thirty, *murgh*=bird in Persian). After the bedraggled flock had waited for what seemed an eternity at the door of the King's palace, a chamberlain emerged to advise them to turn back, for they could never hope to endure the King's glorious presence. The birds insisted on their steadfast desire. At length the servant opened the door and ushered them in. As he vanished from their sight he pulled back a hundred veils. With that "the sun of majesty sent forth its rays, and in the reflection of each other's faces these thirty birds of the outer world contemplated the face of the Simurgh of the inner world."

But their pilgrimage does not end there, for the additional stories of the death of the martyr-mystic Hallaj and the king's sacrifice of his own beloved suggest that their journey *in* God is just beginning.[6] Some four centuries later, Attar's fellow countryman Mulla Sadra (d. 1640) would go on to develop a fascinating and remarkably complex metaphysical system within which to speak of the Path of Enlightenment.

He wrote, "So this is the arrival at the Ka'ba of the ultimate Goal and the encounter with the One Who is worshipped. But it is only possible by traveling rapidly the Way of knowledge on the feet of thought and inquiry. . . ."[7]

Signs Among Believers: Islam as a Unique Faith Community

Important as the notion of a physical, geographical center has been in Islamic tradition, Muslims have always insisted that the centrality of Makka and the pilgrimage thereto yield to larger issues. Finding the center of one's life is no mere ritualistic formality. Numerous texts in the Qur'an make it clear that at the heart of the original message stands the challenge of fostering genuine community, on a foundation of justice and integrity.

> Uprightness is not a question of turning your faces to the *qibla* of East or West. Uprightness means rather believing in God and in the final day, and in the angels and the Book and the prophets. It means sharing your wealth, dear as it is to you [some would translate this phrase "out of love for Him"], with kinfolk, orphans, the poor, the traveler [lit. son of the road], those who come asking, and for setting slaves free. It means performing the ritual prayer (*salat*), giving alms (*zakat*), living up to one's solemn word, and bearing up under the most intense hardship and in dire straits. (Qur'an 2:177)

Chapter 2 discussed some of the natural symbols by which Muslims, as religious persons among others who likewise interpret their experience in religious terms, express their right relation to the cosmos. We turn now to examine some of the distinctively Islamic ways in which Muslims have

Dome mosaics in Great Mosque of Cordova, Spain (c. 961), over the bay that holds the *mihrab* marking the *qibla*, or Makka-facing "direction" of ritual prayer.

expressed their relationships among themselves, thus forging a unique community of faith.

> These are the signs [verses] of the clear Book. We have sent it down as an Arabic Qur'an, so that you might understand. (Qur'an 12:1-2)

Muslims believe, as do Christians and Jews, that the most significant events in human history are those that define *their* history. If the "signs on the horizons" describe the overall terrain in which God reveals himself, the concrete historical fact of the Qur'an, revealed in Arabic over some twenty-three years, marks out the beginning of the "main road" on which Muslims journey as a community. Here the mode of expression becomes distinctively Islamic, a language and symbol-system no longer universal but confessional. Terms of membership in such a community are definitive and exclusive. In a tradition that crosses many ethnic and cultural boundaries, there remains a good deal of latitude in actual practice, but one must make a deliberate choice for or against membership.

How have Muslims defined themselves as a distinct community of faith? What is distinctively Islamic about Islam? Put most simply, to be a Muslim is to adhere to God's revelation in the Qur'an as spoken by the Prophet Muhammad, to proclaim God's absolute oneness and transcendence and Muhammad's definitive prophethood. "We have sent a Messenger into your midst and from among you, to recite to you [literally, make a Qur'an about] our signs . . . and to teach you the Book and the Wisdom." (Qur'an 2:151) The story of how that simple dual affirmation of faith has manifested itself in time and space is much more complex.

During the course of some fourteen centuries, a remarkable variety of cultural and ethnic entities have come to identify themselves as "Islamic." As the influence of the early

Muslims expanded, it became more and more evident that neither the text of the Qur'an nor the paradigmatic words and deeds of Muhammad enshrined in the community's collective memory corresponded item for item with the new issues that surfaced with changing times and circumstances. Nevertheless, Muslims maintained the undiluted conviction that the scripture and the prophetic example (*sunna*) constituted eternally valid guidelines. The enormous challenge was how to adapt and reinterpret those two sources while preserving their pristine authority and integrity. Here we shall unfold a little of the history of how that process gradually translated those signs into Islam's central religious institutions.

For the sake of clarity only—one cannot disentangle such matters without oversimplifying a great deal—we will look at this complex story from two angles. First, under the general heading of "history and models of leadership" we explore some of the implications of Muhammad's position and the crisis that his death precipitated. Second, the notion of "authority and implementation of the sources" will suffice to describe Muslim solutions to the problem of how to translate the earliest Arabian sources into more broadly applicable guidelines. Both considerations will begin with a text from the Qur'an that situates both the Prophet and the scripture in the context of our metaphors of journey, sign and light.

History and Models of Leadership: Caliphate and Imamate

> He [God] is the one who sends manifest signs to his servants, that he might lead you from the depths of darkness into the light. . . . O you who believe! Keep in mind your charge to trust in his Messenger, and he [God] will grant you his mercy doubly. He will provide you a light by

which to walk, and he will forgive you . . . (Qur'an
57:9, 28)

Trusting Muhammad while he lived must have been natural
enough for those who knew him personally. But how could
anyone be trustworthy enough to act as his successor when he
died? Muhammad's death thrust the young community into
a protracted debate over the criteria of legitimate succession.
And that debate gave rise to a diversity of opinion that would
in turn have serious implications for the implementation of
Qur'anic standards, as we shall see shortly.

According to sources compiled as much as two or three
centuries after Muhammad's death in 632 C.E., two predomi-
nant solutions to the problem of succession emerged. One
group maintained that the Prophet had explicitly designated
his son-in-law Ali to be his Caliph (literally, "successor" or
"vicegerent"). The other, convinced that Muhammad had
made no such appointment, opted for the procedure of
choosing from among a group of elder Companions of Muhammad. They chose Muhammad's father-in-law Abu Bakr.
The group that supported Ali's candidacy came to be called
the Shi'a ("party," "supporters") of Ali, popularly known as
Shi'ites. Those who backed Abu Bakr were in the majority
and formed the nucleus of what came to be called the "People
of the Sunna and the Assembly," Sunnis for short. Ali's back-
ers continued to insist that Ali was unfairly passed over three
times, gaining only in 656 C.E. the leadership role that had
been his by right for nearly thirty-five years.

The well-known distinction between Sunni and Shi'i
identifies only the largest institutional division within the
Muslim community. Muslims are quick to point out that
none of these so-called "divisions" indicates any noteworthy
variations in belief and practice among the world's nearly one
billion Muslims. Still, major classical sources from within the

tradition have seen fit to describe their own history in terms of these allegiances. Traditional sources identify several subdivisions within the two major ones. Here is a brief sketch of the two principal Shi'i groups.

Major differences between what have evolved into the two largest segments of Shi'ites began to crystallize around the second half of the eighth century. Until that time, Shi'i Muslims were in general agreement in recognizing the leadership authority of a hereditary succession of six descendants of Muhammad, beginning with Ali and his two sons, Hasan and Husayn. These figures they called Imams. In 765 C.E., Ja'far as-Sadiq, the sixth in that line, died. Again opinion divided over legitimacy of succession. One group had pledged allegiance to Ja'far's older son, Isma'il. When Isma'il died even before his father did, some who had acknowledged Isma'il's succession continued to insist on its validity. Effectively terminating the line with Isma'il, whose death they interpreted as a temporary departure from the scene, this group came to be called the "Seveners" or "Isma'ilis." They in turn eventually divided into more than one subgroup. Seveners today live, for example, in East Africa, Pakistan and India. The largest of the groups acknowledges the Agha Khan as its leader.

According to another interpretation of the events of the 760's, Ja'far the Sixth Imam saw fit to abrogate the designation of the deceased Isma'il by naming a younger son, Musa, as his successor. Those who acknowledged Musa's leadership would follow a line of succession all the way to a twelfth Imam. Their theological interpretation of history says that in about 874 C.E., the twelfth Imam went into a "lesser concealment," a period during which he communicated to his followers through a series of four representatives (*wakil*). In 940 C.E., the last of those spokespersons died without having appointed a successor. Since the Imam was no longer actively communicating, Twelver Shi'ites call that date the beginning of the "greater concealment," a condition that obtains to this day. These Twelvers, also called Imamis or Ja'faris, constitute by far the largest Shi'ite group and account for over ninety percent of Iran's population and just over half the population of Iraq. Twelver Shi'ism became the state religion of Iran in the early sixteenth century.

Both Twelver and Sevener views of history are distinctly millenialist in tone. Though there are some important differences in how they have elaborated their theologies, both have historically looked forward to the return or reemergence of the last (i.e. seventh or twelfth) Imam. He will establish then an age of justice in which all believers will reap the rewards of the redemptive suffering of the Imam's extended family (especially for Twelvers) or from the Imam's healing arcane knowledge (a classical Sevener notion). Sunni tradition also looks forward to the advent of a Mahdi (Guided one) at the end of time, but there the idea is not so fundamental as in Shi'i tradition.

At this point it will help to clarify one aspect of Twelver thought that has given rise, especially since the Iranian revolution, to a caricature of Shi'ites and, by association, of all Muslims. While the concept of the martyrdom and redemptive suffering of the Family of Muhammad (i.e. the Imams) is central to Twelver spirituality, media characterizations of Iranians or Iraqi Shi'ites as suffering from a "martyr complex" are inappropriate. Wherever human beings find some cause for which they would offer their lives, they do so in view of a value that transcends the individual human life. It happens that some people express that transcendent value in terms of patriotism, others in terms of hope of a life beyond the earthly. In either case people simply die for something greater than themselves. In neither case do their choices necessarily suggest a devaluation of human life.

At various times in Islamic history different models of leadership have predominated. By far the single most important has been that of the caliphate. In that model, the successor to the Prophet, the caliph, has ideally served as both political and spiritual leader, Commander of the Army and of the Faithful. After its beginning in Madina and reestablishment for about eighty-nine years in Damascus, Baghdad was the caliphate's center for some five centuries; but the caliphate's authority did not go uncontested. Several rival caliphates laid claims, most notably in Cordova and Cairo (under an Isma'ili Shi'ite dynasty called the Fatimids). In the mid-eleventh century the caliphate suffered a severe abridgment when a Turkic dynasty overcame Baghdad and vested the caliph's temporal power in a new parallel institution called the sultanate. After the Mongols sacked Baghdad in 1258, various dynasties made largely symbolic attempts to prop up or otherwise revive the moribund institution. Nowadays the caliphate is a memory, though some still dream of its resurgence. In practice, a wide range of political institutions, from monarchies to constitutional republics to military dictatorships, now govern predominantly Muslim nations.

In addition, claimants to leadership of the Imamate type arose from time to time. Mahdist movements (Sunni) have been attempted with varying degrees of success until modern times. One abortive attempt at such a movement occurred as recently as 1979, around the beginning of the Iranian revolution and the storming of the American embassy in Tehran. At that time Sunni and Shi'i Muslims alike were observing the beginning of the fourteenth Islamic century. In Tehran Twelvers relived the suffering of Husayn against the evil tyrant in their struggle against the Shah and the United States in regular observances that mark the beginning of every year, but take on renewed importance at the turn of a century. In Makka a small Mahdist group, recalling the tradition that with each new century God would raise up for Islam a "renewer," took over the sanctuary of the Ka'ba. They proclaimed a short-lived new age and paid with their lives for daring to violate the holy place.

Interpreting the Signs: Authority and Implementation of Sources

With that all too brief sketch we must move on to other institutional dimensions of Islamic community that have arisen in the process of implementing the mandate of the revealed sources.

> It is not fitting that God should speak to a human being except by inspiration [a technical term used of revelation given to a prophet], or from behind a veil, or in commissioning a messenger that he might deliver a revelation by God's leave. . . . So by our command we have revealed to you spiritually. You knew neither the scripture nor the faith, but we have made of it [the Qur'an] a light by which we guide whomever we choose among our servants. And it is you who guide to the Straight Path, the Path of God to whom belong what is in the heavens and what is on earth. Do not all things move toward God? (Qur'an 42:51-53)

In the Qur'an, God speaks to Muhammad in a number of such instructions on the nature of revelation. The light of the Book's guidance becomes the primary touchstone against which Muslims must judge the authenticity of their faith in action. Some texts provide explicit regulations regarding matters of personal and social morality as well as ritual practice. On the whole, however, the Qur'an does not function as a legislative handbook. Very early in Islamic history, local communities faced issues on which the book rendered no explicit opinion or ruling. Then as now, the community's most pressing challenge was how to interpret the sacred text so as to preserve its spirit and still respond to changing needs.

While Muhammad lived, problematical lacunae could be more or less instantly filled by the Prophet's ad hoc responses and clarifications of Qur'anic issues. Not long after his death, what had begun as a rather informal process of preservation of Muhammad's utterances in the living memory of Muslims evolved into a more formal development. To prevent the loss of Prophetic tradition, scholars went in search of Hadith (Sayings or Traditions) across the world. Collecting massive numbers of them, they sifted through the material, attempting to sort out the authentic from the spurious. By the end of the ninth century, Muhammad's words and deeds had been institutionalized into a number of written collections, six of which have been considered especially authoritative. These collections of Hadith came to form the second major source upon which scholars would base their decisions on the shape of Muslim life.

From about the late seventh century, the community as a whole began elaborating various interpretative principles and procedures. Schools of legal methodology came into being, each with its own peculiar emphasis on one or another aspect of juristic thinking. As the initially all-Arab Muslim community came into contact with an ever wider range of ethnic groups and cultural settings, the need to be able to address new problems grew. Since each culture and ethnic group the Muslims met already had its own legal and religious history, the Muslims had to find ways to put their stamp on the conquered territory without destroying what they found there. They thus had to learn how to incorporate the "customary" law of the place, extending the umbrella of their own system so as to allow the conquered peoples some latitude of practice.

As one might expect, a city like Madina, whose people considered themselves custodians of the original legacy of Muhammad, would naturally tend toward a more cautious and conservative approach. Meanwhile in territories such as Syria and Iraq, the conquering Muslim armies had been posted as a matter of policy away from the major existing cities, in newly founded garrison towns. Eventually such sites grew into cities of importance in their own right. In Iraq, for example, there were Basra and Kufa; across Egypt and North Africa, there was Fustat near modern day Cairo and Qayrawan in Tunisia. Located as they were in areas more culturally and ethnically diverse than the Arabian peninsula, these cities frequently—though not always—fostered more innovative and flexible approaches to religious issues.

All Muslims agree on the primacy of the Qur'an as the source of revealed truth, and on the importance of Hadith as the principal source of information about the example of the Prophet, the Sunna. Originally most Muslim scholars considered Sunna virtually co-extensive with Hadith: all that one could know, or needed to know, about the Prophet's example, one could find in the collected sayings. Gradually the notion of Sunna expanded to include not only Muhammad's reported words and anecdotes about his deeds, but the actual living practice of a given community of believers. And that growing attitude was in turn based on a Hadith in which Muhammad is reported to have said, "My community will not agree on an error." It followed naturally that the community, striving in good faith to live out the Sunna of the Prophet, literally embodied a living Sunna that already presupposed an interpretation of Muhammad's example. In simple terms, the community strove to live as Muhammad surely would "if he were here now."

With this expanding notion of Sunna we see the beginnings of a third source of religious law, after Qur'an and

Hadith—namely, the consensus or agreed practice of the faithful. Eventually consensus, called *ijma'*, became a technical tool for extending the applicability of the revealed law. If a question arose upon which neither Qur'an nor Hadith made any specific statement, one could seek the solution in the actual practice of the community. The idea is not terribly unlike the classical Roman Catholic notion of *sensus fidelium,* the "conviction of the faithful." It is grass-roots elaboration of how religious persons live out their commitments.

Suppose now that an issue arose upon which neither Qur'an nor Hadith nor actual practice could shed definitive light. What then? In the earliest days of the Islamic expansion, the religious judges (*qadi*) appointed to oversee the ordinary affairs of communities in newly conquered territory were accorded considerable latitude in the exercise of "individual judgment" (*ra'y*). Many scholars were concerned that the practice was too fluid and easy prey to the unbridled use of personal opinion. As a result, the more informal process of *ra'y* was gradually forged into the more rigorous and tightly controlled tool of reasoning called analogy (*qiyas*), somewhat like what lawyers today call argument from precedent. A very rough and overdrawn example of how it might work is this. Suppose a question arises as to the legality of using crack cocaine. Neither Qur'an nor Hadith specifically mentions such a thing, and since it has never before surfaced in the local community, one can find no "living Sunna" about the matter. One can then, as a last resort, appeal to analogy. One major characteristic of crack cocaine is, for example, that it impairs one's rational faculties. Both Qur'an and Hadith make it clear that intoxicants or other substances that produce such results are intolerable. In addition, the practice of the local community has steadfastly refused to allow such destructive behavior. One can therefore conclude, on the basis of the "reason" or "link" between a previously unknown substance and others known to produce similar results, that revealed law condemns the use of crack cocaine. Taken together, Qur'an, Sunna, as enshrined both in the Hadith and the community, consensus and analogical reasoning came to be called the four roots of religious law.

By the end of the ninth century, about the time the major authoritative written collections of Hadith had come into being, several distinctive schools of jurisprudence had formed. Four Sunni schools remain active today. Each traces its origins back to a founding figure. Abu Hanifa (d. 767 C.E.) lived and worked in the Iraqi town of Kufa. His school or *madhhab,* the Hanafi or Hanafite, developed a somewhat greater tolerance for the use of analogy than the other schools. Today the Hanafi is the dominant school in Turkey, India and Pakistan. At the other end of the spectrum stands the school named after Ibn Hanbal (d. 855). A major figure in the religious and intellectual life of ninth century Baghdad, Ibn Hanbal debated with the Mu'tazilites over what he considered their unconscionable elevation of speculative reason to a position effectively above divine revelation. The harder the Mu'tazilites pushed, the harder Ibn Hanbal pushed back, so that the two sides grew further and further apart. When the Mu'tazilites fell out of favor at the caliphal court, the new caliph released Ibn Hanbal from prison. Over the next century or so, the more conservative and traditional approach of Ibn Hanbal became the order of the day. Hanbali influence in our time is limited to the Arabian Peninsula, where it has virtually no competition from other *madhhabs.*

Between the Hanafi and Hanbali schools stand the Shafi-'ite, named after Shafi'i (d. c. 819), and the Malikite, founded by Malik ibn Anas (d. 795). The former functions largely in Southeast Asia and parts of Egypt, the latter mostly in North Africa. On the whole, Islamic jurisprudence seeks to strike a balance between individual and community, both in terms of

Elaborately-carved stone facade of the Seljukid Ince Minare madrasa (1260–65) in Konya, Turkey, with texts from the Qur'an along center and border registers.

needs, rights and responsibilities, and in terms of legislative authority. Shi'i legal scholars also developed at least two major law schools, of which one currently dominates the scene in Iran. That school, called the Mujtahidi, emphasizes the requirement for every Muslim to subscribe to the teaching of a particular living *mujtahid,* a legal scholar authorized to exercise independent legal investigation, called *ijtihad.* Whereas, at least in theory, Sunni legal tradition has claimed that the "door of *ijtihad*" swung closed around 900 C.E., Shi'i jurisprudence has consistently taught the need of ongoing elaboration and reinterpretation. In this context it will be helpful to address at least indirectly some questions many American readers have about how Khumayni's Islamic revolution came into being and about how revolutionary-minded Muslims there view the coalescence of religion and state. Here is a sketch of some major developments.

The history of Shi'ism can be seen as alternating between periods of political quiescence and activism. In the earliest centuries (seventh to ninth), there were "family" revolutions against caliphs and their governors, but then relatively little directly political activity. Sunni dominance toward the late ninth and early tenth centuries may have led to the elaboration of the doctrine of the Twelfth Imam's "lesser concealment" at first, from 874 to 940, with the Imam's will executed by his four "special deputies," and "greater concealment" later, from 940 on, until the return to establish an age of justice. In other words, Shi'ite eschatology may have developed as a justification for political quiescence. The original notion of the rule of the Imam was modified into an eschatological concept of the Imamate as a way of protecting the Shi'ite community by obviating the need for conflict with the Sunni government, on the grounds that any government will do until the Imam returns.[8]

In 1501 the Safavid dynasty, which had its roots in a

once-apolitical religious order, came to power in Iran and established Twelver or Imami Shi'ism as the "state" creed. Over the next two centuries or so, important developments occurred in the growth of a class of religious scholars and authorities.[9]

Three terms most commonly associated with Islamic religious officialdom everywhere are these: *ulama,* a general category that refers to all "learned" in religious matters; *faqih* and its plural *fuqaha,* referring more specifically to those who exercise the formal function of *fiqh,* jurisprudence; and *mujtahid,* a title given to the most eminent of the *ulama* who have proven themselves fit to exercise *ijtihad,* independent investigation into and articulation of religious law. The Shi'i doctrine of the Greater Concealment of the Twelfth Imam required the institution of an authority structure capable of interpreting (fallibly) the mind of the absent (infallible) Imam. Hence, the exalted office of the *mujtahid.* Under the Safavid dynasty (1501–1722), mujtahids were few in number. Over the decades the religious institution witnessed a sort of honorific inflation, so that there are at present various ranks within the category of mujtahid, including two levels of *hujj-atulislam,* "proof of Islam," and two grades of *ayatullah,* "sign of God," accorded by virtue of ability, constituency, etc. Readers who have followed events in the Middle East over the past decade or so have seen these terms often in the press. (See table 2.)

At first the Safavids maintained control over religious officialdom because (1) the shahs claimed, spuriously, descent from the Imams, (2) the religious scholars were imported into Iran and thus beholden to the ruler for their livelihood, and (3) the only important ulama were government-appointed. But the shahs did set up special offices for the religious figures, while decreasing the religious functions of other court officials. Gradually the ulama became more

Table 2.

Shi'ite Hierarchical Structure During Khumayni Era

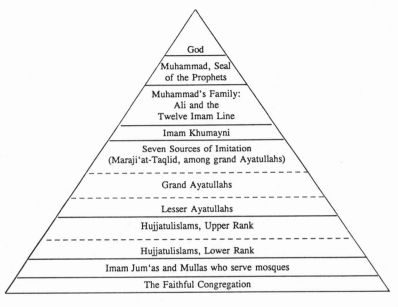

God

Muhammad, Seal
of the Prophets

Muhammad's Family:
Ali and the
Twelve Imam Line

Imam Khumayni

Seven Sources of Imitation
(Maraji'at-Taqlid, among grand Ayatullahs)

Grand Ayatullahs

Lesser Ayatullahs

Hujjatulislams, Upper Rank

Hujjatulislams, Lower Rank

Imam Jum'as and Mullas who serve mosques

The Faithful Congregation

and more independent, financially, because they were increasingly supported by "inalienable pious endowments" (*waqfs*) given either to sustain religious or charitable institutions or as private bequests with ulama acting as executors; and socially, because the teaching that the faithful must follow the most learned mujtahid in the Imam's absence won them growing popular following, especially among the bazaaris (shopkeepers) and merchants.

Eventually, the "non-official" leadership funded by waqfs and gifts outstripped the government-appointed officials, such as the *shaykhulislams*—chief religious functionaries in various cities—and the *imam jum'as*—leaders in the principal mosques in the major cities. Two eighteenth century developments need to be mentioned here. First, political decentralization and tribalism, aridification and increasing nomadism, among other causes, made the Safavid dynasty relatively easy prey to invading Afghans in 1722. The conquerors were Sunni Muslims, so many Shi'i ulama left for the Iraqi shrine cities of Najaf and Karbala, often mentioned during active hostilities of the Persian Gulf War, where they remained independent of Iranian rulers until the 1940s. Second, a brewing conflict between two Shi'i schools of legal thought came to a head. The Akhbaris, who emphasize the Traditions/sayings (*akhbar*) of Muhammad and the Imams, taught the individual's ability to interpret without help from scholars. This is somewhat analogous to the Protestant notion of the priesthood of the faithful and the prerogative of each believer to interpret scripture. The Usulis or Mujtahidis, who emphasize the principles (*usul*) of religious law and the role of the mujtahid, insisted that believers must choose a living mujtahid as "source of imitation" (*marja'-i taqlid*). There can be several such living sources among the leading mujtahids; prior to the Iranian revolution, for example, Khumayni was reckoned as one of seven chief "sources of imitation."

After the triumph of the Mujtahidi school, influence of the religious scholars continued to expand. Under the Qajar dynasty (1796–1925), the ruling of a mujtahid was still considered fallible, but could be regarded as "less fallible" than the decision of a temporal ruler. Independent ulama maintained their Iraqi teaching centers and spoke out often against the Qajar shahs. As one scholar sees it, "the ideological supremacy of the ulama was rarely contested . . . [and] a socio-ideological leadership made of the ulama increasingly the representatives of popular grievances, especially of the urban guildspeople."[10]

Facade of 17th-century royal oratory mosque of
Shaykh Lutfullah, Isfahan, Iran, showing elaborate
floral decor and inscriptions on tile exterior.

The period since the beginning of the Pahlavi dynasty (1925–1979) has witnessed a dramatic "repoliticization" of Iranian Shi'ism. That came to a head when Ruhallah Khumayni returned to Iran to proclaim the end of the Pahlavi dynasty and the beginning of the Islamic Republic of Iran. To get some sense of the imagery that communicated the religious dimensions of the revolution, a picture will help.

Imagine a large colorful poster depicting a confrontation between two familiar figures. On the right and slightly elevated stands Ayatullah Khumayni, his right hand raised in a gesture that suggests the authority to banish a foe. Just below him and to the left, a fire-breathing dragon assaults a fallen and terrified Riza Shah Pahlavi, the second and probably last in the Pahlavi dynasty. Decked in military finery, but with the peacock crown and sword shattered and lying at his side, the Shah reaches desperately over his left shoulder to clutch at the coattail (American flag) of a bearded figure whose top-hat bears a Star of David and whose shirt is the Union Jack. As the saber-toting Uncle Sam moves toward the left and downward into darkness and an inferno of tormented souls in hell, a veiled angel hovers above Khumayni's head in a blaze of light on which are superimposed these verses from the Qur'an: "We [God] said: Do not fear, for you are the uppermost" (Qur'an 20:68); "Go to Pharaoh, for he has transgressed" (20:24); "He [God] said: 'Moses, cast it down,' and behold it was a slithering serpent" (20:19–20). Together to the left of the angel are the verses "On that day those who were unjust will find their excuses of no avail" (30:57) and "For them is the curse and the evil abode" (13:25). With his left hand, the Ayatullah gathers up his flowing outer robe and holds a Qur'an. Standing by itself just to the right of Khumayni's head is the quasi-proverbial line, "For every Pharaoh there is a Moses."

Khumayni thus became the supreme lawgiver whose authority could not be questioned, for he represented the spiritual descendants of Muhammad, the Imams. His interpretation of Shi'ite political theology marked a major departure from the classical doctrine, according to which the religious scholars generally functioned outside of political structures, exercising often the rights of a kind of loyal opposition. The end of the Iran-Iraq war, and Khumayni's death several years ago, brought new challenges to the young revolutionary nation: questions of succession, the preservation of administrative structures in the absence of the charismatic leader, accommodation to the world outside, and so forth.

Responding to Signs Among Believers: The Range of Islamic Tradition

Non-Muslims—and many Muslims as well—often think of the "Islamic world" as a homogeneous entity, uniformly motivated by a world-grabbing impulse to impose Islamic values upon all peoples. All Muslims do not think alike. Table 3 shows several interrelationships among ideas and institutions. From left to right the table has arranged various thematic aspects of Islamic tradition; from top to bottom are a number of possible variations on those themes that a study of Islamic history reveals. Those variations as described here do *not* reflect neatly segregated groups or convictions within the Islamic community. They merely serve as a device by which to suggest the *range* of actual responses that "signs among believers" have elicited from generations of Muslims. Except in the case of the "Sources of Law" and "Schools of Legal Methodology," where the tradition has made fairly clear divisions, it is best to regard the top-to-bottom variations as a spectrum or continuum, a question of emphasis, rather than as a lineup of well defined and mutually exclusive options.

Table 3. The Range of Islamic Tradition

RELIGIO-CULTURAL STYLES	ACCESS TO TRUTH	SPIRITUALITY QUALITIES EMPHASIZED	SCOPE OF HUMAN ACTION	SOURCE OF MORAL VALUATION	SOURCES OF LAW	SCHOOLS OF LEGAL METHODOLOGY
Fundamentalist: Qur'an = unalterable standard literalist, politically active; revive spirit of Prophet's days, w/o intervening Medieval interp.	Scriptural Revelation	Transcendence Servanthood	God foreordains all: Sovereignty, Power, etc.	Theistic Subjectivism: God's command confers value on acts	Qur'an	Hanbali
	Prophet Muhammad	Imitation of Ideal Exemplar		*(Sources)*	Hadīth	Shafi'i
Conservative: Accepts all worthy achievements, views change w/much caution; politically passive	Community	Conformity, w/Implicit trust in Collectivity Acting in Good Faith	Limited freedom & responsibility	Muhammad's example or "Agreed Practice" of Comm.	Sunna — Ijmā' *(Method)*	(=taqlīd)
						Maliki
Adaptationist: Reinterpret Qur'an & Sunna re: changing needs; political pragmatism	Reason	Intelligent Faith, with Personal Conviction		Rational Objectivism: God commands/forbids because inherently Good/Evil	Qiyās (Analogical Reasoning)	Hanafi
Personalist: Subordinates legal/communal institutions to leader/personal piety; politically active	Divinely guided mediator/charismatic leader	Immanence, strong affect	Acts freely chosen, emp. accountability	Good/Evil in terms of higher goal: rel. to God or obedience to Imam	Qur'an/Sunna as interp. by Imam/shaykh	Mujtahidi Shi'i

Those options would be better displayed visually if one could arrange them in a circle instead of a straight line.

Religio-Cultural Styles: A study of Islam's history and scope reveals first a range of what we will call "religio-cultural styles," suggested by several overall approaches to Islam's sources.[11] If one's only acquaintance with Muslims came via the news media, one might think all Muslims were "radical extremist fundamentalists." Unfortunately, when non-Muslims hear the term "fundamentalist" so used, they often translate it as "lunatic fringe." Fazlur Rahman, a noted Muslim scholar, clarifies the term by defining fundamentalism as an active force standing midway between "conservative placidity and the uncontrolled pioneering adventures of liberalism." Properly understood, Islamic fundamentalism developed during the eighteenth and nineteenth centuries as a protest against the "Westernism" Rahman defines as "the projection of Western (i.e. purely secular) modernity into non-Western societies."[12] Searching for greater precision, interpreters sometimes use such alternate terms as "neo-normative," "integralist," or "revivalist." A common characteristic of this style, known by whatever name, is a literalist reading of the Qur'an, whose absolute validity remains pure, universal, and unconditioned by historical circumstances. Paradoxically, however, the style has often encouraged highly original and imaginative scriptural exegesis, and virtually demands the exercise of *ijtihad* in the elaboration of law. Politically activist, the approach seeks to recapture the spirit of the golden age of the Prophet and adapt it to contemporary needs, thereby establishing a society purged of centuries of irrelevant medieval interpretation that has side-tracked Muslims from their original destiny. The Muslim Brotherhood, now gaining popularity in Egypt and Jordan and elsewhere in the Middle East, is one example of the approach.

"Conservative" (other terms used include also "normative," "orthodox") fairly describes the style that likely characterizes the vast majority of Muslims. Cautious and suspicious of all major change, this approach prefers to let stand the full record of Muslim history. Because it tends toward political passivity, it has generally preferred even leadership judged deficient by Islamic religious norms to revolution and anarchy.

The "Adaptationist" (also called "acculturationist" or "Modernist") style favors fresh interpretation of Qur'an and Sunna in terms of changing needs. It takes a rather pragmatic view of politics, recommending leadership models on the basis of utility rather than Islamic legitimacy. Adaptationists encourage the incorporation of non-Islamic contributions to world culture while at the same time raising Muslim consciousness about Islam's pioneering role in civilization.

Finally, the "Personalist" (or "charismatic") style places the role of the inspired leader above all religious institutions, in fact if not in theory. Like the fundamentalist style, this approach also leans toward political activism and, if necessary, revolution to bring about its version of a just Islamic society. Contemporary Iran represents a good example of the style, especially under Khumayni. In the history of Muslim religious institutions one finds the approach represented particularly in Sufi religious orders (about which we shall say more in Chapter 4). Those organizations originally developed around charismatic figures of legendary sanctity, called shaykhs, whose directives members accepted in blind obedience. The history of Christian religious orders offers numerous parallels.

Access to Truth: Muslims agree unanimously that the Creator has made truth available to humankind preeminently in the scriptural revelation called the Qur'an, and in the life of the Prophet Muhammad. But in addition, Muslims have historically sought to discover truth through the secondary or subsidiary avenues: in the good faith practice of the community of believers, in the application of reason, and in the leadership of charismatic figures believed to be divinely guided. No one style pursues only one avenue, but the various approaches do have their characteristic emphases, as the chart suggests. The majority of Muslims have rejected the Mu'tazilite adaptationist style, for example, because it seemed to accord speculative reason an authority higher than that of revelation. Many Muslims likewise reject the personalist approach because of a tendency to set up a human being in the role of mediator between God and humankind.

Spirituality: Each style also manifests a preference for certain spiritual attitudes or qualities. Once again, all Muslims would agree that a believer is first and foremost a servant of the transcendent God, desirous of following in the footsteps of the Prophet. A certain uncritical nostalgia can accompany an idealization of the Prophet and his era, and Muslim historical sources brim with suggestions that things have only deteriorated since the golden age. But beyond that, Muslims—like most folk, it seems—value a certain level of spiritual likemindedness, characterized by an attitude of simple confidence that God is guiding the collectivity of believers along the Straight Path. At its best, this can produce a stong sense of community and solidarity; at its worst, it can yield stolid conformity. Personal conviction along with an intellectually keen assessment of the human condition very clearly informs the personal quest of countless Muslims, whether or not they would dream of calling themselves "adaptationists." Finally, a sense of divine immanence and intense affect often characterize the personalist dimension. Of course millions of Muslims every day are moved to tears as they pray and experience God forgiving and moving and living in their hearts. But among some segments of the Muslim population—Shi'ites for example—heightened affective expression has historically been evident.

Scope of Human Action: Muslims have taken a variety of approaches to the question of human freedom and responsibility. On the whole, Islamic statements on the subject tend to describe rather what God is than what human beings are not. In other words, the statement that God "guides to his light whom he will" is meant to underscore God's absolute power and transcendence, not to hint that human beings have no choice and are therefore not accountable for their actions. The chart simply indicates the full spectrum of positions, without intending to associate one or the other definitively with any one group or style. Nevertheless, some Muslim writers have in recent times observed a correlation between social and cultural stagnation and the dominance of the notion of predestination, with its corollary that human beings have no control over their lot in life and might as well be resigned to their fate.

Source of Moral Valuation: Islamic thought evidences a range of ideas as to how one can assess the moral value of a human act. At one "end" of our circular spectrum is what one could call "theistic subjectivism." According to that view, God in his sublime liberty decides what is good and evil and labels all things accordingly, informing humankind via the revealed law. Murder is evil because God decrees it so, not because of any intrinsic quality in the act. Further along the continuum is the notion that the good is what Muhammad modeled by his behavior and/or what the community of Muslims have validated in good-faith practice. Evil is everything else. Still further along is "rational objectivism," analogous to a natural law position. According to this view, God commands some actions and forbids others because they are inherently and of themselves either good or evil. In other words, God says "Thou shalt not kill" because murder is essentially evil, as any being endowed with reason will readily discern. Lastly, the notion that good and evil are defined by some higher goal has played a significant role in Islamic history. That "higher goal" is often expressed as either one's personal relationship to God or unquestioning obedience to a supreme leader or a spiritual guide. Such a view runs the risk of degenerating into either personal antinomianism or large-scale unquestioning acceptance of a leadership that regards itself beyond the pale of moral accountability.

The remaining columns in the chart simply set out the fundamentals of Islamic religious law we discussed above. While the sources or "roots" and schools are distinct enough in themselves, their arrangement in relation to the material in the other columns is meant only to suggest some general affinities. For example, the Hanafi law school historically has resorted more readily to the use of qiyas (analogical reasoning) and on that score alone shows some kinship with the adaptationist style. Similarly, the Mujtahidi school is uniquely Shi'ite and thus relates in a general way to the style most characteristic of Shi'ite Islam, namely the personalist.

An in-depth analysis of Islamdom as a unique community of faith would require far more space than we have here. One can scarcely reduce a tradition of such antiquity and depth to a few broad characterizations such as these. Inadequate as it is, this little survey must suffice to provide the larger context within which to locate the spiritual prospects and aspirations of millions of individual Muslim seekers after God. A saying popularly attributed to Muhammad states, "Anyone who denies God's decree is an unbeliever, but anyone who claims he does not sin is a liar." It expresses vividly the need to strike a balance between belief in God's absolute control over all affairs and the awareness that each human being remains responsible and cannot claim that his or her actions were simply predetermined. Keeping in mind that natural tension between needs and rights individual and communal, and between qualities and prerogatives divine and human, we turn to a consideration of what Islamic tradition has to offer the individual as a spiritual path.

Questions for Discussion

1. How many different ways have Muslims interpreted the meaning of Hajj? What parallels can you find in other religious traditions? What are some similarities and differences between Islamic pilgrimage practices and, say, those of Hindus or Buddhists? Why is pilgrimage such a powerful and apparently universal symbol?

2. What makes a place like Makka sacred? What might a study of sacred space and place in the Islamic tradition suggest about the larger topic of sacred geography in the history of religions? What are some symbolic meanings of "Ka'ba" in Islamic tradition? Can you think of any parallels in Christianity or Judaism?

3. Where do Muslims look to find direction in their journey as a community of faith? How has Islam's history been an ongoing interpretation of those signs? Do you see indicators of the social implications of religious belief?

4. What are some of the major religious institutions that have developed in Islamic history? What are the principal models of religious leadership? What implications do they have for modern political developments? How might one best describe the differences between Shi'i and Sunni branches of the Muslim community? Can you think of any parallels in other religious traditions?

5. How would you describe the range of Islamic tradition? What are some of the major intellectual and ethical issues to which a variety of approaches have been evident in Islamic history?

Dome of the Rock, Jerusalem. Built 692.

4

Isra'/Mi'raj: Signs Within the Self and the Individual Spiritual Path (Tariqa)

Islam's presence on the world scene, both in relation to the larger human community and as an exclusive community of faith, has been and remains imposing and of crucial importance to the future of the human race. In its vision of the world as well as in its religious institutions and ethical demands upon its adherents, Islam is truly a name to conjure by. To the individual, as well as to the collectivity, Islam likewise has much to say; for it has been far more than the institutionalized mass religious culture that has formed the impressions of and the bulk of the imagery passed along by and to most Westerners. Islam's tradition of spirituality and personal guidance runs deep and broad. This chapter looks first at the paradigmatic experience of Muhammad's Night Journey and Ascension, at the "signs within the self" and the "Science of Hearts" that has helped individuals to interpret them, and at the irreducibly personal realities each Muslim must prepare to face at journey's end.

Isra'/Mi'raj as Metaphor for the Spiritual Life

At the center of the Temple Mount in Jerusalem stands a magnificent domed octagonal structure known as the Dome of the Rock, for centuries associated with tales of Muhammad's Ascension and with the intriguing visionary allusions in Qur'an 53:13-18. According to traditional interpretations, that text's references to Muhammad's apparent vision of a figure at the marge of the next world, marked by another of those mysterious cosmic trees, must be taken as a hint of the ineffable experience of Ascension that followed upon the Prophet's journey from Makka to the site of Solomon's Temple. Details added by generations of storytellers include colorful descriptions of an odyssey through the seven heavens, in each of which Muhammad meets a particular prophet, and of his glimpses of Hell's torments. Some of Islam's finest poets and miniature painters have celebrated these accounts in word and image.[1]

The intent of the tradition is clearly both to emphasize further Muhammad's association with, and preeminence among, earlier prophets, and to make a statement of Islam's hegemony in the city sacred to Jews and Christians. Politically the Dome of the Rock, and the later association of the nearby Al-Aqsa mosque with the Night Journey, are part of a message of conquest. From a religious and spiritual point of view the implications are paradoxically both broader and more focused.

Ascent, understood as a generic concept, naturally provides a metaphor for explanations of the dynamics of spiritual growth. In the opinion of the great mystic Rumi, speech and action are the dusty road of one's outward journey, while the inner journey takes the spirit beyond the heavens. Rumi elsewhere describes human life as an upward evolution in which a series of deaths and rebirths lead from the mineral to the vegetable to the animal to the human to the angelic, and finally to the stage at which God alone exists. At that point one must again speak, as Attar did in Chapter 3, of the journey in God. Rumi is convinced, as are other Muslim mystics through the ages, that one finds the clue to humanity's true destiny not in the "water and clay" of the body, but in the "divine secret" of the pure soul.[2]

In a more explicit way, Muhammad's course has become a model for the aspirant as well as for the spiritually adept. Bayazid al-Bistami, who appeared in Chapter 3, first recounted his own experience as a parallel to that of Muhammad. In his collection of biographical sketches of holy personages, *Recollections of the Saints,* Farid ad-Din Attar records Bayazid's description of his approach to the Throne of God. The last part suggests the extent to which Muhammad's proximity to God had become the ultimate exemplar of spiritual development.

> Then my spirit transcended the whole Dominion, and Heaven and Hell were displayed to it; but it heeded naught. Whatever came before it, that it could not suffer. . . . When it reached the soul of God's Chosen One [i.e. Muhammad] . . . there it beheld a hundred thousand seas of fire without end, and a thousand veils of light. . . . I desired to be able to see but the tent-peg of the pavilion of Muhammad, I had not the boldness. Though I had attained to God, I had not the boldness to attain to Muhammad.
>
> Then Abu Yazid said, "O God, Whatsoever thing I have seen, all has been I. There is no way for me to Thee, so long as this 'I' remains; there is no transcending my selfhood for me. What must I do?"
>
> The command came, "To be delivered out of thy thouness, follow after Our beloved, the Arab Muhammad. Anoint thine eye with the dust of his foot, and continue following after him."[3]

Recognizing that no one can or will ever duplicate Muhammad's experience, the mystical tradition nevertheless models descriptions of the spiritually adept person's experience upon that of Muhammad. Hujwiri (d. 1074), author of one of the earliest theoretical analyses of the tradition, makes this distinction: "The ascension of prophets takes place outwardly and in the body, whereas that of saints takes place inwardly and in the spirit."[4] Bayazid's description of his own ascension enumerates ten stages: ascent to heaven, presentation before God, gifts of clothing and adornment, crowning, being called God's chosen beloved, being seated on God's Throne, knowledge of God's deeds, drinking from the divine cup, union with God, and return to earth on a mission.[5]

Signs Within the Self and Setting Out on the Path

Few Muslims would consider themselves worthy even to aspire to Bayazid's experience. Indeed, Bayazid got himself into a great deal of trouble for daring to describe his spiritual journey so boldly. Today some Muslims virtually disown the entire mystical tradition, arguing that people like Bayazid and the somewhat later Baghdadi mystic al-Hallaj (d. 922) were presumptuous to the point of blasphemy. The mystics, however, were merely drawing out what they took to be the implications of such Qur'anic verses as, "Wherever you turn, there is the face of God" (2:109) and "We are nearer to the individual than the jugular vein" (50:16). A saying attributed to the Prophet says, "Who knows oneself knows one's Lord." Some mystics interpreted the Hadith "as a condensation of the basic experience of the mystical path as a way inward, an interiorization of experience, a journey into one's own heart."[6] Whether or not an individual Muslim qualifies as a mystic, the important point is that the overall tradition allows considerable scope for the seeker who longs to know, and be known more intimately by, God. Sufi sources attribute similar sayings to God himself (Sacred Hadiths). For example: "I fulfill my servant's expectation of me" and "Though the heavens and the earth cannot contain me, there is ample room for me in the believer's heart."

For most Muslims the process of traveling toward union with God has been less spectacular and very much a day to day struggle. But that is precisely what Bayazid was trying to say, albeit in fairly esoteric terms, when he suggested that each individual is indeed granted an ascension on the "Buraq of self-forgetfulness." Buraq was the winged quadruped that bore the Prophet heavenward; "self-forgetfulness" translates *fana'*. A central concept in the mystical tradition, *fana'* refers to the ultimate goal in the realization of one's servanthood, the loss of self before the absolute being of God.

Muslim spiritual writers have long made a distinction between wayfarers, by far the majority of seekers, and those who are "drawn" to God as though by a powerful force from outside themselves. The wayfarer (*salik*) God guides along an active, purgative way, through long periods of prayer and asceticism. Beginning with awareness of the effects of God's actions in the world—what the Qur'an calls "signs on the horizons"—the wayfarer is led upward to the divine names. From there the traveler moves still higher to the contemplation of God's attributes or essential qualities, and finally to the divine essence itself. A seeker whom God "draws" (*majdhub*) moves quickly and effortlessly, beginning at the divine essence and descending to creatures. The wayfarer finds God in creation; the one drawn sees creation in God.[7] Let us look now at how Islamic tradition has understood the requirements and characteristics of the individual's spiritual life.

Parallel to the Main Road of the Shari'a, along which Muslims walk as a community, is the Path (*Tariqa*). Attar has described the situation this way:

O heart, if you go seeking along this Way, Look carefully
in front and behind, and only then proceed! Look at the
travelers who have arrived at this threshold. Generation
after generation have arrived together! How do you know
about which road to take? How can you know about
which one leads to his threshold? For every single particle
there is a particular entrance: Yes, for each particle there
is indeed a separate road to Him![8]

The Science of Hearts:
Reading the Signs Within the Self

Within the "terrain" of creation, God lays open the main
road of the Muslim community's unique and exclusive history. Believers discover and set out on that road in the company of others. Community supports the individual's desire
to acknowledge God's signs, for God has created an affection
among the hearts of believers such as all the riches on earth
could never effect (Qur'an 8:63). In the end, nevertheless, it is
the solitary heart that must make and continually renew the
choice.

Individual persons experience as a personalized gift the
light of faith that God casts into the heart. One scholar describes it as "an inward personal experience, more or less
transitory as an event but enduring in relevance, which is felt
to express or lead to a special authoritative and normative
relation between the individual and cosmos."[9] Here we shall
look at how the Islamic tradition has provided means of practical guidance for every seeker desirous of that.

By way of background, it will be helpful to sketch the
development of the principal institutions associated with the
phenomenon known as Sufism. Very early in Islamic history,
assorted individuals in such diverse cities as Madina, Damas-

cus and Baghdad became known for their personal piety. Some of course considered them merely eccentric, and others felt these people were going against a Hadith that seemed to rule out such "monk-like" practices (though there are other Hadiths in which Muhammad is reported to speak highly of certain forms of asceticism).

Out of the early ascetical movement, which arose partly as a protest against the increasingly regal style of the caliphs, there grew the beginnings of mysticism. Around the end of the eighth century there lived in Basra, Iraq a woman named Rabi'a; she would become the first great mystical poet who dared speak of her loving relationship with God. Within a century, more such poets appeared, speakers of Persian as well as of Arabic, all over the central Middle East. Gradually small groups of seekers began to cluster around these and other holy persons. Such informal circles were the beginnings of what would later develop into formally constituted religious orders, the first of which appeared in the eleventh century under the famous and still widely popular shaykh Abd al-Qadir al-Jilani (d. 1166). The term *tariqa* or "personal spiritual path," originally used to describe the individual's search for God, came to refer to the formal orders. Each seeker thus became an aspirant, an initiate, and an adept within a particular Tariqa. As in the Christian tradition, many of the orders grew and spread rapidly, some splitting into sub-orders and establishing their own variant of the original founder's charism.

Groups at first small enough to meet and even take shelter in the homes of the shaykhs and shaykhas (female spiritual guides) eventually outgrew those accommodations. Thus were founded the first Sufi architectural designs intended to provide for all the formal and functional needs of the orders: residential, ritual, and social, including libraries and soup kitchens. They are called variously *zawiya, khanqah, tekkiye.*

Many such foundations eventually included a funerary function, beginning as the burial places of founders and later serving as cemeteries for subsequent shaykhs and administrators of the orders.

Within that institutional framework, the Sufi mystical tradition developed a number of spiritual disciplines and exercises designed to aid the traveler in keeping to the Path. As Muhammad needed the guidance of Gabriel on his passage to the Unseen World, so does every individual require some assistance in interpreting the signs within the self.

Through every stage of the journey that will admit of description, ongoing contact with a spiritual guide is of utmost importance. Spiritual direction and discernment developed to a fine art in Islamic tradition. Certainly not all contemporary Muslims, or even a substantial minority, seek out individual spiritual direction. If they did, they would be largely frustrated in their search, for the active practice has fallen off dramatically since its heyday. But one can still find in various parts of the Muslim world a practice equivalent to "group spiritual direction."

Surviving along with a number of formerly more highly visible religious orders is the gathering of seekers for a prayer service (known as *dhikr*) that often involves ritual recitation of the Qur'an, chanting of mantra-like words and phrases in Arabic, and dancing. In Cairo, for example, during festivities honoring holy personages such as members of the Prophet's family, one can find groups of people engaging in ritual dancing and chanting. After many such ceremonies, members gather around the shaykh (the leader of the order) for spiritual conversation. Members raise a wide range of issues for discussion, and the shaykh responds with his considered reflections on the matter, drawing on the rich trove of ancient wisdom handed down from one generation of adherents to another. To one such gathering several years ago in Istanbul,

Gathering of Sufis in Istanbul, 1988. Shaykh at right center facing camera.

several visiting American guests were invited. During the talk after prayers, one of the guests told the interpreter she thought the shaykh was a wise and holy man. The shaykh responded modestly through the translator, "You are looking at a mirror," and proceeded to elaborate on how, as Muhammad had said, "The believer is mirror to believer." In those remarks that so summed up the spirit of the occasion, the fortunate guests had gotten a small taste of Islamic spiritual direction in action. But if the actual practice of individual spiritual direction has fallen into desuetude, the interested Muslim can find an extraordinarily rich collection of classical sources that have enshrined the tradition for centuries and that wait to be rediscovered.[10]

To assist wayfarers both to name their experiences of God's action in their lives and to give some structure of their understanding of the discipline their quests demand, early Muslim theoreticians devised a system of "psycho-spiritual typologies." Those spiritual masters noted that some interior movements and conditions come and go quickly and evidently with no effort on the part of the seeker, while others abide and apparently arise at least in part from human effort. They called the former "states" (*hal, ahwal*), and the latter "stations" (*maqam, maqamat*). Authors vary somewhat in their analyses and in the resulting catalogues, and differ as to the number of states and stations, the order in which they occur, and the particular features that characterize and identify one or other level of spiritual growth. Although these typologies do not envision or recommend some sort of rigid sequence, most do suggest a sort of "ladder" by which the aspirant can emulate in some small way the heavenward journey of Muhammad.

Since stations remain longer, one can more readily observe and enumerate them. The numbers seven and forty have especially potent associations in this context. We mentioned earlier the notion of "the prophets of one's being" as symbols of spiritual development. Those prophets number seven in the system devised by the Persian writer Simnani (d. 1336), paralleling the number of valleys through which Attar's thirty birds must struggle, and to the number of heavens in the story of Muhammad's Ascension. Some authors list as many as forty stations. One such inventory gives an idea of how one might envision the wayfarer's progress: intention, conversion, repentance, discipleship, spiritual struggle, constant attention, patience, invocation, contentment, opposition to the lower self (the "Greater Jihad" to which we shall return shortly), equanimity, surrender, confidence or trust in God, asceticism, worship, abstention, sincerity, truthfulness, fear, hope, loss of self, survival in God, knowledge of certitude, genuine certitude, intimate knowledge, effort, sanctity, love, ecstasy, nearness, meditation, union, unveiling, service, catharsis, solitude, expansion, assent to the Truth, the supreme goal, and, finally, Sufism. The author of that list concludes his treatise by observing that, "Of these stations, each belongs to one of the prophets . . . the first Adam and the last Muhammad. . . ."[11]

In addition to the practice of individual spiritual direction, that of a retreat of forty days has likewise held a place of esteem in classical sources. Traditions connected with three of those prophets form the basis for the considerable importance of the forty day retreat in the history of Islamic spirituality. According to Qur'an 7:142, Moses fasted forty days and nights. Had he not thus separated himself from worldly concerns, he would have been unfit to converse with God as he did. Another tradition says that God kneaded the clay of Adam for forty days, each day representing a "veil" between humanity and God. Finally, in order to demonstrate Muhammad's unrivaled proximity to God, Muslim mystics put into

God's mouth the saying "I am Ahmad [a title of Muhammad] without the 'm.' " The resulting word is *ahad,* Arabic for "One." As Annemarie Schimmel explains, the letter "m" has a numerical value of forty and therefore corresponds to the forty stages that span the gap between divinity and humanity. "M" is "the letter of creatureliness and trial, of discontinuity and limitation, of death . . . and of the illusory aspect of everything besides God."[12] The arresting saying thus emphasizes Muhammad's relationship with God while simultaneously differentiating between God and his creaturely prophet.

A seeker who submits to the unique discipline of the forty day retreat (*chilla, khalwa*) may, God willing, experience a remarkable renewal of the spirit. In Maneri's words, "When the forty days have drawn to a close, all the veils will have disappeared and much knowledge and mystical illumination will simply be poured into" the retreatant.[13] In a literary work based on the experience of the forty day retreat, Attar personifies the thoughts of the meditator as a wanderer through the cosmos who makes forty stops in search of guidance. The traveler begins with Gabriel and several other angels and proceeds through conversations with Heaven, Hell, plants, animals, Sun, Moon, Sea, Earth—including virtually all the elements and minerals. Eventually he meets and speaks with seven prophets in succession. After conversing with Muhammad (station thirty-five), this pilgrim of the imagination comes at last to the ocean of Soul. Here begins a journey that the poet says defies all description, for it is the same journey in God upon which the thirty birds embark once they have discovered the Simurgh.[14] As a rule, the retreat is so effective that, in Maneri's words, "If . . . wisdom does not show its face to somebody who has completed a forty-day retreat, then it is clear that he has fallen into some negligence in observing its requisite conditions."[15]

Personal Prayer and the Ethical Demands of the Path

Alongside the practice of the five daily ritual prayers, offered in concert with millions of others, the Islamic tradition recommends a variety of private devotional or "free" prayer, usually called by the generic term *du'a,* or supplication. The best prayer is any that Muhammad first pronounced. Even the angels took their cue from the Prophet. A favorite prayer of Muhammad's was one he recommended that Muslims pray on their pilgrim way to Makka:

> O God, indeed you know and see where I stand and hear what I say. You know me inside and out; nothing of me is hidden from you. And I am the lowly, needy one who seeks your aid and sanctuary, aware of my sinfulness in shame and confusion. I make my request of you as one who is poor; as a humbled sinner I make my plea; fearful in my blindness I call out to you, head bowed before you, eyes pouring out tears to you, body grown thin for you, face in the dust at your feet. O God, as I cry out to you, do not disappoint me; but be kind and compassionate to me, you who are beyond any that can be petitioned, most generous of any that give, most merciful of those who show mercy [a reference to Qur'an 12]. Praise to God, Lord of the universe. Amen.[16]

Some prayers come directly from the Qur'an. Chapter 1 mentioned, for example, a Hadith that extolled the Throne Verse as the most excellent of prayers. Like the Throne Verse, many popular prayers acknowledge the divine unity and praise God's majesty and transcendence. Prayers of praise are often very short, meant to be repeated in mantra-like fashion. The great medieval pastoral theologian al-Ghazali, ever attentive to the needs of ordinary people in search of words, suggests a list of ten phrases. He recommends any combination that will total one hundred repetitions:

> 1) there is no god save God alone, he is without partner, his is the kingdom and his the praise, he makes live and causes to die, yet he is ever living and never dying; from his hand comes all good, and he has power over all things; 2) there is no god save God, the king, the truth, the evident; 3) there is no god save God alone, the victorious, the Lord of the heavens and the earth and what is between them, the almighty, the forgiving; 4) glory be to God, praise be to God, there is no god save God, God is great, there is no power nor might save with God, the high, the mighty; 5) glorious and holy is the Lord of the angels and the spirit; 6) glory be to God, praise and glory to God the almighty; 7) pardon me, God almighty, apart from whom there is no god, the living, the steadfast, I beseech thee for repentance and pardon; 8) O God, none withholds what thou givest and none gives what thou withholdest, none opposes what thou ordainest, good fortune does not benefit its possessor, apart from thee; 9) O God, bless and preserve Muhammad and the house of Muhammad and his companions; 10) in the name of God, along with whose name nothing harms either in earth or in heaven, he is the hearing, the knowing.[17]

Sometimes one cannot find the appropriate words for prayer; perhaps no words at all come trippingly to the tongue. In moments like that, heart's desire and mind's intent more than make up for whatever else seems lacking. Rumi tells a marvelous tale about a pious Muslim who made haste one Friday toward the mosque. Muhammad was leading the community in the congregational prayer that day, and the man was particularly eager to be there with them. Arriving at the mosque, he found a crowd emerging and asked why they were leaving early. They replied that he was simply too late, for Muhammad had just dismissed them with a blessing. At that the man heaved such a sigh of frustrated longing that his heart smoked ("sigh" is "heart-smoke" in Persian). One of those just leaving the mosque noticed the sigh and was so taken by it that he said, "I will trade you all of my formal prayer for that one sigh of yours." The late-comer agreed to the swap. Later that evening as the bargainer went off to sleep, a voice assured him, "You have bought the water of life and healing. To honor your choice, I accept the ritual prayer of all my people."[18]

Rumi tells another story about a man who prayed devoutly, keeping vigil late into the night. Once when he began to tire and weaken in his resolve to persevere, Satan saw his chance and planted a suggestion in his weary soul: "For all your calling out 'O God,' have you ever once heard God reply 'Here I am' "? The man had to admit he had never detected even a faint whisper in reply. God took note of all this and sent a messenger to the praying man. All of the fear and love the man had poured into his invocation, the messenger assured him, were already God's gift, unrequested and unrealized. "Beneath every 'O Lord' of yours lies many a 'Here I am' from me." No one seeks God but that God has first planted the desire to seek; the answer is prior to the question.

In prayer as in so many other dimensions of the spiritual life, Abraham sets the example. Rumi notes that where there is no sighing, there is no ecstasy; and Abraham was the "sighful man" par excellence. When the patriarch prayed, his personal commitment and intensity caused his heart to bubble. You could hear Abraham praying for miles.[19]

Chapter 1 spoke of the overwhelming sense of God's majesty and transcendence that one finds in texts like the Throne Verse. Islam's treasures of personal prayer speak with equal power of God's intimate presence. The ninth century

Egyptian mystic Dhu 'l-Nun (d. 859), a man renowned as quite a colorful character, speaks of his experience of God in the "signs on the horizons."

> O God, I never hearken to the voices of the beasts or the rustle of the trees, the splashing of waters or the song of birds, the whistling of the wind or the rumble of thunder, but I sense in them a testimony to thy Unity, and a proof of thy incomparableness; that thou art the all-prevailing, the all-knowing, the all-wise, the all-true, and that in thee is neither overthrow nor ignorance nor folly nor injustice nor lying. O God, I acknowledge thee in the proof of thy handiwork and the evidence of thy acts: grant me, O God, to seek thy satisfaction with my satisfaction, and the delight of a Father in his child, remembering thee in my love for thee, with serene tranquillity and firm resolve.[20]

The martyr-mystic al-Hallaj describes his awareness of God as he reads the "signs within the self."

> O God, the sun neither rises nor sets but that your love is one with my breathing. Never have I sat in conversation, but that it was you who spoke to me from among those seated round. Never have I been mindful of you, either in sadness or rejoicing, but that you were there in my heart amidst my inmost whisperings. Never have I decided on a drink of water in my thirst, but that I saw your image in the cup.[21]

Elsewhere Hallaj says God is so close as to "flow between my heart and its sheath as tears flow between eye and eyelid." Islamic tradition abounds with examples of that intimation of divine immanence. One famous Sacred Hadith has God say,

> My servant comes ever closer to me through works of devotion [i.e. other than those prescribed as religious

duties]. When anyone comes toward me a hand's breadth,
I approach an arm's length; if anyone comes toward me
an arm's length, I approach by the space of outstretched
arms; if anyone comes toward me walking, I will come
running. Then I love that person so that I become the eye
with which he sees, the ear with which he hears, the hand
with which he takes hold. And should that person bring
to me sins the size of the earth, my forgiveness will be a
match for them.[22]

Attendant upon the personal relationship with God expressed in these and other such splendid prayers are stringent
ethical demands. Since humankind freely accepted the Lordship of the Creator and the Trust of creation, each person has
inherited responsibility for the shape of things and for the
care of brother and sister. The key to understanding God's
dealings with the individual is the "light cast into the heart."
That light illumines the individual's life only if the person is
disposed to allow it, and then it does so gently. The light
never blinds, and one can always prefer the darkness of doubt
and refusal to trust. Oddly enough, it is only when one delib-
erately tries to force God's hand that one loses control of
one's own destiny. Numerous texts in the Qur'an suggest that
God never wrests effective power of self-determination from
the individual. "We turn a person whichever way he wants to
turn" (Qur'an 4:115 according to F. Rahman's interpretation). "God does not change a people's state until they change
what is within themselves." (Qur'an 8:53; see also 13:11) The
scripture's insistence on the need to seek forgiveness unceas-
ingly suggests the personal freedom to change.

The essential sin is that forgetfulness of God, the heed-
lessness that can gradually stifle the voice of conscience until
it becomes but a "distant call." (Qur'an 41:44) Forgetfulness
of God leads directly to forgetfulness of one's inmost self.

Remembrance of God (*dhikr*) effects personal integration and balances the tension between power and powerlessness, hope and despair, knowledge and ignorance, freedom and determinism. Prospects for the individual in Islam are thoroughly positive so long as one grants the need for reverent awe in God's presence, so long as one acknowledges that God's mercy will overcome his wrath. God will burden no person beyond his or her capacity to persevere. Islam rejects the notion of redemption because human beings are directly responsible. Adam and Eve sinned, but humankind has not inherited their guilt. No human action makes the slightest personal difference to God; the moral quality of each individual's choices turns on their ultimate benefit to the human race. It is not God, therefore, but the individual who decides his or her own final destiny. Those who make their choices in this life in isolation from the needs of the human community as a whole will fashion their own hell hereafter. Those who delude themselves into thinking that their choices have created mountains will see them reduced to a particle of sand. One of the terms the Qur'an frequently uses to describe greed, selfishness, and sinfulness generally, is "going nowhere fast" (*dalal,* aimlessness, wandering in error). If hell is the recognition of the futility of selfishly motivated deeds, heaven is the realization that one's choices were consistent with an enlightened interpretation of the signs on the horizons and within the self.[23]

All Things Perish, Save the Face of God

The ultimate personal challenge is surely the process of coming to face mortality. It is virtually impossible to appreciate the deepest values of another cultural or religious tradition without taking account of its ways of helping its people to approach death. Here we shall examine three dimensions of the Islamic understanding of human mortality. We turn first to the foundations, the Qur'an and Sunna; next, we look at popular belief and practice; and finally we come back around to some samples of how several famous Muslims have negotiated the rapids of their own mortal end.

Nearly all of the Qur'an's many references to death refer at least indirectly to the omnipotence of the God who "Brings to life" and "Causes to die" (two of the ninety-nine names). One of the earliest references relates directly to the content of Muhammad's preaching and the refusal of his listeners to accept it: they have committed spiritual suicide. All unbelief amounts to inner death. Unbelievers scoff and insist they will suffer only the "first death" of the body when their predetermined span of life is done. Only a fool would believe in the "second death" of eternal damnation. In reply the Qur'an insists that in the Fire one neither lives nor dies; all who end up there will beg for death. The Qur'an's imagery of the double death is very similar to that of some Latin, Greek, and Syriac Patristic literature.

Most of the relevant texts concern physical life and death in relation to God's power. As exhortatory devices in Muhammad's preaching, they remind that God's absolute dominion over life and death can give the believer unshakable confidence. God's purposeful control over lifespan, as opposed to the arbitrary and despotic control the pre-Islamic Arabs had attributed to impersonal "Time" or "Fate," leaves the believer free to attend to life as it happens, in the conviction that life is not pure chance but part of a great design. God's providence gives the believer hope in the resurrection, for God will not suffer creation to come to naught.[24]

The Hadith likewise include many ethical-eschatological images. One anecdotal saying of Muhammad has him telling his listeners how Death itself will be slaughtered, leaving the

Taj Mahal, Agra, India. One of the world's
most celebrated funerary monuments.

people of Paradise uninterrupted delight and the people of the Fire no hope for an end to their misery:

> Death is brought in in the guise of a black-and-white-spotted ram. Then a caller calls: "O People of Paradise!" And they crane their necks and look, and He [God Himself] says: "Do you recognize this [figure]?" They say: "Yes, that is Death." And each of them sees him. Then He calls: "O people of the Fire!" And they crane their necks and look, and He says: "Do you recognize this [figure]?" They say: "Yes, that is Death." And each of them sees him. Thereupon he is slaughtered. Then He says: "O people of Paradise! Eternity without death [is yours]! O people of the Fire, Eternity without death [is yours]."[25]

A number of Hadiths are as much instructions on how to live as on how to die. "Die before you die," the Prophet advises; let preoccupation with self pass away now, so that when death comes you will have handed over already that which you fear most to lose. "As you live, so shall you die; and as you die, so shall you be raised up." Therefore, leave your good deeds behind when you go and your good deeds will be your traveling companions on your journey after death. Some sayings about death are blatantly contradictory. Weep for the dead, do not weep for them; weep for only one day, weep for an extended period; the more you weep, the more suffering the dead will feel from the pain of separation, weep to help them with your sympathy; and so forth. What is important here is simply that tradition attributes to the Prophet the complete range of responses to death and mortality.[26]

Every major creedal statement formulated by the early theologians includes statements about death, and specifically about the "punishment of the tomb" and the angelic interrogators who question the deceased about their lives and deeds. Both features seem to arise from Hadith that suggest the dead retain their perceptive faculties. According to one Creed, body and soul are reunited in the tomb; infidels will surely suffer there, and believers who have sinned may also suffer. In any case, even the obedient believer will experience the "pressure" of the tomb. But, according to a Hadith, no punishment will be inflicted on a Muslim who dies on Friday, and the pressure will last only an hour. The Qur'an mentions neither the interrogating angels, Munkar and Nakir, nor the pressure and punishment of the grave. These traditional elements gradually became more detailed and embellished and have become, to some degree, articles of faith.[27]

Before a burial, mourners gather in a mosque, or in front of the deceased person's house, or in a specially constructed enclosure, to pronounce the *takbir* ("God is Supreme," *Allahu akbar*) four times. Although the *takbir* is part of all Muslim prayer and begins the call to prayer itself, its prominence in the funeral rite is such that saying the *takbir* is equivalent to saying "this person (or thing in other contexts) is dead to me," that is, I have surrendered this to God. All attention falls on God's grandeur so that nothing else can distract.[28]

Loneliness is among the most feared sufferings of the tomb. Prayers popular throughout the Islamic world make this very evident. The idea that the spirit returns to the body in the grave serves to heighten the apprehension that the deceased will experience a terrible solitude and acute pain of separation. Referring to Middle Eastern contexts, Constance Padwick explains, "When the great solidarity of family groups and neighborhood groups in Arabic lands, and the very general lack of privacy from birth to death, is considered, this fear is the more understandable."[29]

Prior to leaving the grave, mourners instruct the deceased how to reply to the interrogating angels. They recall the fundamentals of the faith and counsel the departed not to let the angels intimidate, for they are after all also merely creatures. A final graveside prayer from Egypt says:

> O God, Thou Companion of every lonely one, Thou Present One who art never a stranger, Thou Near One when others are far, be the Companion, O God, of our loneliness and his [the deceased's] loneliness, have mercy on our strangeness and his strangeness, and whiten his page [i.e. forgive sin] and forgive us and forgive him and forgive the one who stood over his grave to say: "There is no god but God, and Muhammad is the Messenger of God."[30]

Many believe that after the burial they may apply the merit of their prayers toward the mitigation of the grave's terrors.

Shortly after Muhammad's death, his successor, Abu Bakr, is reported to have addressed the crowd keeping vigil outside the house in Madina: "If you worship Muhammad, know that he is dead; if you worship God, know that he lives forever." According to conflicting Hadiths, Muhammad both encouraged and forbade Muslims to visit his tomb. Most pilgrims to Makka opt for the positive tradition and go to pray at the Prophet's grave. A popular belief that salvation is assured to anyone who dies at or en route to the pilgrimage goal is no doubt enhanced by the inclusion of Muhammad's tomb among the customary sites of the pilgrim's circuit.[31]

Most Muslims will die without having the opportunity to visit Muhammad's grave, but few will lack the blessing of a symbolic presence of the Prophet at theirs. The following prayer Muhammad is said to have offered at the funerals of early Muslims is still in use, as are many others like it:

> O God, forgive the living among us and those of us who have died; those present and those absent; the small and the great among us; our women and our men. O God,

make alive with grateful surrender [lit. islam] whomever among us you cause to remain alive; and cause to die in the faith whichever of us you cause to die. O God, do not keep from us the reward awaiting the deceased, and do not make life hard for us with this passing.[32]

In many parts of the Islamic world the fifteenth day of the eighth lunar month, Sha'ban, calls for special reflection on human mortality and remembrance of the dead. According to tradition, the tree of life is shaken on the eve of that day. On the leaves are written the names of the living, and all whose leaves fall in the shaking will die during the next year. Of course, no one alive knows whose leaves have fallen; so many people take the occasion to offer prayers like this Shi'ite petition:

Have mercy on me on the day when I come before Thee alone, my gaze turned towards Thee, my deeds tied round my neck, all creatures dissociating themselves from me, yes even my father and my mother and those for whom I toiled and strove. Then if Thou dost not show me mercy who will have mercy upon me? . . . Who will teach my tongue to speak when I am alone with my deeds, and am asked concerning those things that Thou knowest better than I?[33]

Surely the single most important communal observance of death and its ultimate significance occurs in the Shi'ite commemoration of the martyrdom of Husayn, who died at the Iraqi site of Karbala in 680 while confronting the evil caliph Yazid. Beginning on the first day of the first lunar month, Muharram, Shi'ites participate vicariously in Husayn's redemptive suffering and death. A ten day observance includes various penances, self-flagellation, processions of mourning, and culminates (at least in more traditional areas) in the "passion play" of Karbala. Scenes in the elaborate drama vary with locality, but always inculcate aspects of the paradigmatic sufferings of earlier prophets such as Abraham, Noah, and Moses.

In the finale the actors play out Husayn's tragic death; grandfather Muhammad persuades Husayn not only to forgive, but to intercede on behalf of, his murderers. "The re-enactment of the drama becomes the occasion for celebrating the crucial meaning of religious death, setting humanity's ultimate value within a transcendent framework, and amplifying the positive aspects in the community's death conceptions. Death, even tortured death, is full of the highest spiritual favor."[34] Sunni Muslims place far less significance on Husayn's death, but veneration of saints and small pilgrimages (*ziyara*) to their tombs are still common in many places.

One can find no more eloquent reflection on the mystery of death than in the writings of the great religious poets. Though they may seem at first to be dodging the grim reality by spiritualizing it into metaphors of mystical annihilation in God, these poets know whereof they speak. Every seeker is counseled to meditate on death as the only path toward reunion with God. Rumi reflects in one of his lyric poems about the prevalent fear of the grave's loneliness. He concludes that even in the tomb the true Lover is never far from the Beloved.

> Look on me, for I shall be your companion in the grave on
>   that night when you pass across from shop and house.
> You will hear my greeting in the tomb, and you will be
>   aware that not for a moment have you been veiled from
>   my eyes . . .
> On the hour when we light the lamp of the intellect, what a
>   tumult of joy shall go up from the dead in the tombs!
> The dust of the graveyard will be confounded by those cries,
>   by the din of the drum of resurrection . . .

On whatever side you gaze, you will behold my form,
   whether you gaze on yourself or towards that uproar
   and confusion.[35]

Maneri believed one attains the summit of spiritual growth
only when one no longer desires either life or death, but is
resigned to accept whatever God gives.[36] A prime example of
that ideal is Abraham. Attar tells this charming story.

When the Friend of God came to die, he was reluctant to
deliver his soul to Azrael [angel of death]. "Wait," he said
to Azrael. "Has the King of the Universe asked for it?"
But God . . . said to Abraham: "If you truly were my
friend, would you not wish to come to me? He who re-
grets giving his life for his friend shall have it torn from
him with a sword." Then, one of those present said: "O
Abraham, Light of the World, why will you not give up
your life with good grace to Azrael? Lovers in the Spiritual Way [lit. tariqa] stake their lives for their love; you set
store on yours." Abraham said: "How can I let go my life
when Azrael has put his foot in the way? I disregarded his
request because I thought only of God. When Nimrod
cast me into the fire and Gabriel came to me, I disregarded him because I thought only of God. Seeing that I
turned my head from Gabriel [who had come to *prevent*
the prophet's death], can I be expected to give up my soul
to Azrael? When I hear God say, 'Give me your life!' then
it will be worth no more than a grain of barley. How can I
give my life to someone unless he asks for it?"[37]

And Unto God Is Your Return: Coming Full Circle

When all is said and done, one has to understand progress along one's own path of return to God within the larger
context of world and religious community. Gifts bestowed on

the individual—the signs within the self—must open one's eyes still more attentively to the big picture. Once again, Muhammad has set the tone. Sharafuddin Maneri offers one interpretation of the ultimate significance of this third paradigmatic journey for the lives of Muslims. Maneri quotes Qur'an 17:1 ("Blessed be He who carried His servant by night . . .") and explains that it was precisely because Muhammad was a *servant* that he was so exalted. The Prophet was "taken to the stage that even the imagination of Gabriel, despite his three hundred thousand feathers, did not reach!" Still Muhammad did not allow his lofty spiritual status to blind him to his fundamental mission. As Maneri explains it,

> the Lord of prophecy [Muhammad] said, at the time that dominion and power were bestowed on him, "I do not want to become a king and a prophet; I want to be a servant and a prophet!" The inspirer of courage placed his service at the gate of the heavenly court—he preferred service to dominion in both worlds. "His eye did not blink, nor did it exceed the limit." (Qur'an 53:17)[38]

The Qur'anic text here cited refers to Muhammad's response to the experience of travel in the Unseen World. Maneri takes the words metaphorically to mean that Muhammad neither shied away from the experience nor succumbed to hybris.

Let us return to where we began our consideration of that central Islamic document, the Qur'an. Chapter 1 paid particular attention to three texts, the Opening sura (*al-Fatiha*), the Verse of Light, and the Throne Verse. Here we shall conclude by looking briefly at some ways in which classical Muslim writers have interpreted those texts in reference to the individual's spiritual journey. Pursuing our controlling metaphor, one might think of the Qur'an's opening sura as the point of departure along the Straight Path, of the Verse of

Light as source of direction, and of the Throne Verse as an expression of the ultimate goal.

In his interpretation of Surat al-Fatiha, Rumi likens the five daily ritual prayers to the five senses, and the "seven verses" to the secret recesses of the human heart, the distillate of its most intimate longings. He further explains the sura's inner meaning in terms of a distinction traditionally attributed to God himself. According to a Sacred Hadith, God told how he had divided the prayer "in two halves, between me and my servant." The first half contains the servant's praise and glorification of God. The second half, God explained, "is between me and my servant, and my servant shall have what he asks."[39] Rumi captures a sense of the cyclical nature of the human spiritual quest in a metaphor of the changing seasons. Following up on hadith's partition of the sura, Rumi cloaks the "servant's half" in garden imagery. As the hopeful petition of all creation the prayer is reminiscent of the cosmos' natural response to its creator.

> "You alone do we serve" is the garden's winter prayer; "From you alone do we seek help" it says when spring arrives; "You only do we serve" means I have come as a beggar to your door—open delight for me and leave me not in sadness. "From you alone do we seek help" means O Helper, I am broken with over-abundant fruit—keep watch over me.[40]

Reflecting poetically on the Verse of Light's spatial and directional connotations (recall the niche in the Makka-ward wall of each mosque), Rumi calls the human heart the mosque where body worships, the Farther Mosque in Jerusalem to which God carried Muhammad by night, and even the Ka'ba. In other words heart is the inner *qibla* to which the individual turns in prayer. Taking the metaphor still further,

Rumi, along with other mystics, likens the body to the niche of which the Verse of Light speaks, and the heart to the lamp within the niche.[41]

The Throne Verse likewise provides a popular metaphor of ultimate goal for the mystics. As in Rumi's interpretations, the microcosm of the person finds a parallel in the macrocosm of the creation, the heavens and the earth. The colorful character Bayazid al-Bistami sums up the essence of the individual spiritual journey admirably. Recall that it was Bayazid who first took Muhammad's Ascension as the model for his own interior odyssey. Bistami reflects on his own life and sums it up this way:

> At the beginning I was mistaken in four respects. I concerned myself to remember God, to know him, to love him and to seek him. When I had come to the end I saw that he had remembered me before I remembered him, that his knowledge of me had preceded my knowledge of him, his love towards me had existed before my love to him, and he had sought me before I sought him.
>
> I thought I had arrived at the very Throne of God and I said to it: "O Throne, they tell us that God rests upon thee." "O Bayazid," replied the Throne, "we are told that he dwells in a humble heart."[42]

Origin, orientation, objective—it is impossible to separate them. To paraphrase the words of T.S. Eliot, "In our end is our beginning."[43]

Questions for Discussion

1. How many different ways have Muslims interpreted Muhammad's central mystical experiences, the Night Journey and Ascension? How have they influenced Muslim attitudes toward Jerusalem? How might they be seen together as

a metaphor for the individual spiritual quest? Can you find parallels in the experience of foundational figures in other religious traditions?

2. What is the meaning of the expression "signs within the self"? How have Muslims devised methods for interpreting those signs? What religious institutions have developed as a result? Are there analogies in other traditions?

3. How does Muslim personal prayer suggest an experience of God's immanence or closeness? In what way does Muhammad's example relate to the practice of personal prayer? How does the individual Muslim's religious commitment translate into moral responsibility?

4. How does Islamic tradition describe the end of the human journey? How do Muslim attitudes toward death compare with those taught by other traditions, such as Buddhism, Hinduism, Judaism, Christianity? What role does Muhammad's example play in this regard?

5. How do Muslims view the prospects of a life beyond this one? How can one best prepare for that final transition? How does the example of Muhammad help Muslims to put earthly life in perspective?

Epilogue: Islam in America: Last Leg of a Global Journey

Imagine yourself a visitor to Washington, D.C. In such a cosmopolitan capital, you naturally expect to see all around you evidence of connections between the United States and other cultures. Still, you cannot help being surprised when, as you stroll down Embassy Row, you come suddenly upon the Islamic Center, a handsome structure in an Egyptian neo-classical architectural style. Now imagine yourself driving north toward Detroit along Interstate 75. Just south of Toledo the view on your right opens up to reveal a dazzling white structure set on a slight rise, with a central dome flanked by two rocket-like minarets. No, you have not taken a wrong turn and landed in Istanbul. You have, however, seen a vision of both the present and the future of Islam in the United States.

The Islamic centers in Washington, D.C. and Perrysburg, Ohio are but two of the more physically impressive institutions of their kind that have appeared on the American landscape over the past several decades. Such centers of Muslim identity now number between six and eight hundred, and some estimates range as high as a thousand. Most are quite simple and ordinary in appearance, for they are merely converted residences, buildings that once housed small businesses, or even former Christian churches and schools. More and more these places are becoming a concrete indication of the growth of Islam as an American religious tradition. At their present rate of growth, Muslims will in twenty-five years

Islamic Center of Greater Toledo, Perrysburg, Ohio.
Turkish style architecture.

constitute the second largest faith community in the United States. Estimates as to the numbers of Muslims vary from around one to nine million. Whatever the actual count, it is clear that Islam is no longer "over there somewhere."

Unfortunately, the growing presence of Islam in this country frightens many Americans. They have, as suggested often in earlier chapters, come to associate the very mention of Islam with strangeness and mystery and, alas, violence. The challenge now facing many American non-Muslims is that of understanding our Muslim neighbors as fellow citizens and brothers and sisters in the human race. The facts of religious and social change invite us all to stretch our notions of who and what "belongs" in our land. Americans have generally been very good at rising to that challenge.

Turning specifically toward Islam and our Muslim neighbors, it may help first of all to answer the question, "What goes on in those Islamic centers?" The answer in general is simply: very much the kinds of things that go on in churches and synagogues. Their primary function is that of mosque (Arabic *masjid,* literally place of prostration), though most manage to make room for a wide range of activities. As mosques they need first of all to provide for their members' ritual needs, including especially a place to perform the ablution before *salat.* But both because the development of secondary institutions needs time and financial resources, and because Islam has always adapted to its surroundings, American Muslim centers now house a range of functions long accommodated especially in churches. Muslims respond to the same needs for religious education, fellowship, and fund raising. Some of the older and better established centers include specific facilities for the broader range of activities. Perrysburg, for example, has a large room adjacent to the prayer hall for meetings and presentations, as well as a full kitchen and eating facility on the lower level for social gatherings. Plans call for a large expansion, including a separate educational wing and residential capability. Together these places of prayer and social gathering represent the collective aspirations of Muslims in America to establish a community of faith and values in which family and social solidarity can flourish.

Islam's American Journeys

How did Islam take root on this continent? Much the same way Judaism and Christianity did, except that Islam *may* have gotten here sooner. What is certain is that some early slaves from West Africa, and perhaps as many as twenty percent of African slaves brought during the eighteenth and nineteenth centuries, were Muslim. Because they were slaves, these early Muslims had little chance to nurture the spread of their faith in any formal ways. That process would begin only in the late nineteenth century with an influx of mostly Arab Muslims from the Middle East. The period between the two world wars saw a second major migration; a third commenced just after World War II and continued for some twenty years. Unlike earlier immigrants, who had sought wealth that they could take back home later, those who came in subsequent waves were often fleeing political oppression. With requirements for entry to the United States stiffened in the mid 1960s, the most recent phase of immigration has included well educated Muslims from a variety of countries, and notably from South Asia (India, Pakistan, Bangladesh).

A second aspect of Islam's growth in America is its presence among African-Americans. The story is one of fascinating sectarian developments especially over the past fifty years or so. Most readers will have heard of the "Black Muslims," and many non-Muslim Americans still think that when one refers to American Muslims, one means those African-Americans once associated with Elijah Muhammad. Formal identification by African-Americans with things at least nominally Islamic dates back to early this century, with Noble Drew Ali's founding of the Moorish-American Science Temple. Remnants of the movement that began in Newark can still be found here and there, its male members including the Turkish term for a nobleman, Bey, as part of their religious names.

A much more important development began in Detroit during the 1930s. There a little-known character named W.D. Fard offered African-Americans a way of identifying with their African roots: their ancestors had been Muslims and it was time to rediscover their heritage. When Elijah (Poole) Muhammad joined the group, "The Lost-Found Nation of Islam in the Wilderness of North America," Fard bestowed upon him the mantle of prophetic office. Elijah's message had little in common with basic Islamic teachings and amounted to a form of reverse racism. Still the Nation of Islam, the group's shortened title, offered the benefits of an enhanced sense of dignity and worth and many positive community-building values.

One of the Nation's most famous members was Malcolm (Little) X. The most formative influence on Malcolm X was his pilgrimage to Makka. There he found that, contrary to Elijah's message of racial segregation and black superiority over white, everyone "snored in the same language." Malcolm returned full of a conviction of human equality, eventually disavowed Elijah Muhammad's teachings, and was assassinated in 1965. Malcolm's dissent deeply influenced Elijah's son Wallace, and when in 1975 the elder Muhammad died, Wallace began the process of sweeping reforms with the intention of bringing the community into line doctrinally with mainstream Islam. That involved a frank repudiation of Elijah's most cherished views. Taking the religious name Warith Deen (close to the Arabic for "heir to the religion"), the new leader would lead the community through a series of changes of name and identity over the next eight years. Its name was changed to the American Bilalian Community, and its newspaper was called *Bilalian News;* for tradition has it that the Prophet Muhammad chose as his *muezzin* an Abyssinian named Bilal, the first black convert to Islam.

Now those whose roots go back to Elijah Muhammad have divided into two main groups. The majority followers of Warith Deen have come more and more to be integrated into the larger American Muslim community, while followers of Louis Farrakhan still identify themselves as the Nation of Islam and carry on the separatist spirit of Elijah Muhammad. The majority of African-American Muslims no longer consider themselves a distinct religious society and have dropped such former names as World Community of Islam in the West and American Muslim Mission.

One last small contingent of American Muslims is made up of indigenous, mostly female, white converts. Some become Muslim so as to share the faith of a spouse, but many women say they find Islam attractive because they believe it accords women greater dignity than American society in general. A still smaller number of Americans consider themselves as least secondarily or incidentally Muslim by virtue of their belonging to "Sufi" groups whose founders trace their spiritual lineages back to various of the mystical organizations mentioned in Chapter 4. I used the terms "secondarily or incidentally" because such groups often place greater emphasis on human unity than on exclusive membership in an Islamic faith community.[1]

Signs on the American Horizons

Somewhere not far away there are Muslims seeking to find their way among their fellow Muslims and Americans. What might they take for the critical signs? Where are they looking for guidance and values? And whither might they see their personal paths unfolding before them? In general they might find that they share with many Jews and Christians deep concerns about the future of life in this country. They seek ways to practice their Muslim faith to the fullest, ways that still allow them to participate in American life without becoming ghettoized. It is a major challenge to maintain one's religious identity in a society so secularized as ours, a society in which there is often so little conviction as to the dignity of persons, a society in which transcendent values so readily lose their place to the ephemeral and the quick fix.

Some Muslims find ready parallels between the Makka of Muhammad's time and the America of our own. In an increasingly stratified society, the rich get richer, the poor poorer and more numerous. Women, children, and a host of minorities struggle for their rights, often without effective advocacy in the corridors of power. Long term solutions to problems threatening the custody of the earth and its wealth are set aside in favor of economic expediency. Most difficult of all, perhaps, some Muslims find that because fellow Americans perceive them as not only "different" but as a presence to be feared, they are not entirely welcome. Muslims want not to be automatically assumed to have ties with terrorist groups, or to be uniquely partial to public beheadings or the stoning of adulterers. They, like all of us, wish merely to be accepted on their own terms as persons. As Muslims become more and more integrated into the larger religious scene in this country, they will most definitely also become more involved in state and national political processes. As we have discussed in other contexts earlier, the Hijra is not a thing of the past. As in Muhammad's experience, so perhaps also in that of millions of American Muslims, life is best seen as a cycle of journeys, continually leading outward and then back to the center and greater self-understanding for the individual within community, and then beginning all over again.[2]

***

Muslim and non-Muslim Americans alike now find themselves struggling to interpret terrible and disturbing signs on their horizons. Many Muslim Americans face major challenges as never before. Their challenges include finding ways to continue cultivating the rich cultural patrimonies they and their parents cherish while integrating their practice of Islam into a whole new cultural context. They face the daunting task of striking a delicate balance between active support of the global community of Muslims, many of whose suffering they feel keenly, and allegiance to the land they have chosen to call home. Speaking out against distortions of their tradition will be the most demanding *jihad* ever for America's moderate Muslims. Current events challenge all Americans, of whatever persuasion, to seek greater perspective on the economic and geo-political aspects of our membership in the human race. Failing that, America's still-insatiable appetite for the planet's finite supplies of fossil fuels will, unfortunately, continue to dominate American foreign policy decisions, promising to entangle us again and again in exploitative relationships to nations like Kazahkstan, whose populations are predominantly Muslim.

Notes

Chapter 1

1. Rudolf Otto, *The Idea of the Holy* (New York: Galaxy, 1958).
2. William McKane, *The Book of Fear and Hope* (Leiden: Brill, 1962), pp. 57ff.
3. M. Ayoub, *The Qur'an and its Interpreters* (Albany: SUNY, 1984), p. 248.
4. From the Persian of Sana'i's *Hadiqat al-Haqiqat,* I:2–11.
5. Yusuf Ibish, "Ibn Arabi's Theory of Journeying," in Y. Ibish and P.L. Wilson, eds., *Traditional Modes of Contemplation and Action* (Tehran: Imperial Iranian Academy of Philosophy, 1971), pp. 441–446. For more on the subject, and on Ibn Arabi's "prophetology," see William Chittick, *The Sufi Path of Knowledge* (Albany: SUNY Press, 1990), and R.W.J. Austin, trans., *The Bezels of Wisdom* (Mahwah: Paulist Press, 1980).
6. See, for example, S.H. Nasr, *Ideals and Realities of Islam* (London: Allen and Unwin, 1966), for related observations.
7. Further see M. Watt, *Muhammad in Mecca, Muhammad in Medina* (Oxford: Oxford University Press, 1953, 1956).
8. K. Cragg, *The Mind of the Qur'an* (London: Allen and Unwin, 1973) and *The Event of the Qur'an* (London: Allen and Unwin, 1971).
9. M. Ayoub, *The Qur'an and Its Interpreters* (Albany: SUNY Press, 1984), p. 251.

10. H. Gatje, *The Qur'an and Its Exegesis* (Berkeley and Los Angeles: University of California Press, 1976), pp. 146–47.
11. Ayoub, *op. cit.,* p. 249.
12. H. Gatje, *op. cit.,* pp. 243–45.
13. Ayoub, *op. cit.,* pp. 250–51.
14. Jn 21:25, Revised Standard Version.
15. New American Bible.
16. Henry Corbin, *The Man of Light in Iranian Sufism* (Boulder: Shambhala, 1978) pp. 121ff on the "Seven Prophets of Your Being."
17. *Mishkat al-Masabih,* James Robson, trans. (Lahore: Sh. M. Ashraf, 1975), pp. 488–89.

Chapter 2

1. Muhammad Yusuf Faruqi, "The Hijra and its Normative Significance: A Glance in Historical Perspective," in *Hamdard Islamicus* 12:4 (Winter 1989), pp. 3–14, quoting from p. 4.
2. Robson, *op. cit.,* pp. 16 and 1123.
3. John Renard, *The Prophetology of Jalal ad-Din Rumi* (unpublished Ph.D. dissertation, Harvard, 1978), pp. 187–88; Annemarie Schimmel, *Mystical Dimensions of Islam* (Chapel Hill: University of North Carolina, 1975), p. 222. See also Qur'an 9:40.
4. Thanks to Mark Woodward for the suggestion about Southeast Asia.
5. *Islam and Revolution: Writings and Declarations of Imam Khomeini,* Hamid Algar, trans. (Berkeley: Mizan Press, 1981), pp. 382–83.
6. Faruqi, *op. cit.,* p. 11.

7. For a discussion of a broad range of related issues, see Roger E. Timm, "Divine Majesty, Human Vicegerency, and the Fate of the Earth in Early Islam," *Hamdard Islamicus* 13:1 (Spring 1990), pp. 47–57, including in the notes a good selection of bibliography for further reading. Other scriptural texts in Qur'an 2:163–64, 22:18, 30:22–27, 41:37–39, 45:16.

8. Sayyid Mahmud Taleghani, *Islam and Ownership,* Ahmad Jabbari and Farhang Rajaee, trans. (Lexington: Mazda Publishers, 1983), p. 153.

9. *Ibid.,* p. 77.

10. *Ibid.,* p. 88.

11. Summarized from N. Keddie, *Iran: Religion Politics and Society* (London: Frank Cass, 1980), pp. 119–38.

12. *Islam and Revolution,* pp. 181–82.

13. See Homa Katouzian, "The Aridisolatic Society: A Model of Long-term Social and Economic Development in Iran," in *International Journal of Middle East Studies* 15:2 (May 1983), pp. 259–81, esp. pp. 272ff. Also further see *Society and Economics in Islam: Writings and Declarations of Ayatullah Sayyid Mahmud Taleghani,* R. Campbell, trans. (Berkeley: Mizan Press, 1982).

14. *Islam and Revolution,* p. 257.

15. H. Katouzian, "Shi'ism and Islamic Economics: Sadr and Bani Sadr," in N. Keddie, ed., *Religion and Politics in Iran* (New Haven: Yale, 1983), pp. 145–65. For a selection of Bani Sadr's work, see J. Donohue and J. Esposito, eds., *Islam in Transition* (New York: Oxford University Press, 1982), pp. 230–35.

16. M. Fischer, *Iran: From Religious Dispute to Revolution* (Cambridge: Harvard University Press, 1980), pp. 157–58. For a sample of current Muslim thought on the matter of "interest taking," see e.g. M. Siddieq Noorzoy, "Islamic

Laws on Riba (Interest) and their Economic Implications," *International Journal of Middle East Studies,* 14:1 (February 1982), pp. 3–17. For an excellent survey of major issues along with a very extensive bibliography, see Muhammad N. Siddiqi, *Muslim Economic Thinking: A Survey of Contemporary Literature* (Leicester: The Islamic Foundation, 1981). See also Seyyed Vali Reza, "Toward a Philosophy of Islamic Economics," in *Hamdard Islamicus* 12:4 (Winter 1989), pp. 45–60.

17. "Islam and the Challenge of Economic Development," in Donohue and Esposito, eds., *Islam in Transition,* pp. 219–20.

18. For text selection see A. Rippin and J. Knappert, ed. and trans., *Textual Sources for the Study of Islam* (Totowa: Barnes and Noble, 1986), pp. 80–82.

19. Text quoted from C.G. Weeramantry, *Islamic Jurisprudence: An International Perspective* (New York: St. Martin's Press, 1988), p. 172.

20. Text reprinted in *Hamdard Islamicus* 2:4 (Winter 1979), p. 98.

21. See Hodgson's *The Venture of Islam* (Chicago: University of Chicago Press, 1975), esp. vol. 3.

22. Text reprinted in Weeramantry, *op. cit.,* pp. 176–83.

23. Further detail in Weeramantry, *op. cit.,* pp. 113–27. For a sample of recent Muslim writing on the subject, see S.M. Sayeed, "Human Rights in Islam," in *Hamdard Islamicus* 9:3 (Autumn 1986), pp. 67–75; M.M. Ahsan, "Human Rights in Islam: Personal Dimension," in *Hamdard Islamicus* 13:3 (Autumn 1990), pp. 3–14; Amjad Ali, "Al-Qur'an and Human Rights (Individual-Social)," in *Hamdard Islamicus* 12:3 (Autumn 1989), pp. 29–39; Rais ud-Din Khan Sherani, "Muhammad—the Greatest Law-Giver and an Epitome of Justice and Compassion," in *Hamdard Islamicus* 12:4 (Winter 1989), pp. 61–71; Syed Nawab

Haider Naqvi, "Economics of Human Rights: An Islamic Perspective," in *Hamdard Islamicus* 4:2 (Summer 1981), pp. 31–51.

24. For general background as well as greater detail, see Weeramantry, *op. cit.,* pp. 134ff; Majid Khadduri, *The Islamic Law of Nations: Shaybani's Siyar* (Baltimore: Johns Hopkins Press, 1966); *idem, War and Peace in the Law of Islam* (Baltimore: Johns Hopkins Press, 1955); Riffat Hassan, "Peace Education: A Muslim Perspective," in *Education for Peace,* eds. Haim Gordon and L. Grob (Maryknoll: Orbis, 1987), pp. 90–108; Karl-Wolfgang Troger, "Peace and Islam in Theory and Practice," in *Islam and Christian-Muslim Relations* 1:1 (June 1990), pp. 12–24; Obaidullah Fahad, "Principles of Diplomacy in Islam: Privileges and Immunities," in *Hamdard Islamicus* 12:3 (Autumn 1989), pp. 41–48.

25. Ghulam Haider Aasi, "The Qur'an and Other Religious Traditions," *Hamdard Islamicus* 9:2 (Summer 1986), pp. 65–91. See also on Muslim-Christian dialogue R. Marston Speight, *Christian-Muslim Relations: An Introduction for Christians in the United States of America* (Hartford: NCCCUSA Office on Christian-Muslim Relations, 1986); Jane D. McAuliffe, *Qur'anic Christians: An Analysis of Classical and Modern Exegesis* (Cambridge: Cambridge University Press, 1990); and Maurice Bormans, et. al., *Guidelines for Dialogue Between Christians and Muslims* (Mahwah: Paulist Press, 1990).

Chapter 3

1. An excellent primary source dealing with these and various other spiritual aspects of pilgrimage is Letter Six in

Letters on the Sufi Path by Ibn 'Abbad of Ronda, J. Renard, trans. (Mahwah: Paulist Press, 1986), esp. pp. 112–17.

2. Annemarie Schimmel, *The Triumphal Sun* (London: Fine Books, 1978), pp. 93, 291, 318, 325; see also her *As Through a Veil: Mystical Poetry in Islam* (New York: Columbia University Press, 1982), p. 197; and J. Renard, *Flight of the Royal Falcons . . . ,* pp. 210–11.

3. *Sharafuddin Maneri: The Hundred Letters,* trans. Paul Jackson, S.J. (New York: Paulist Press, 1980), p. 134.

4. Translated from Arabic text in A.J. Arberry, *Mystical Poems of Ibn al-Farid* (London: Chester Beatty, 1954), pp. 39ff.

5. *Image and Pilgrimage in Christian Culture* (New York: Columbia University Press, 1978), p. 33.

6. *The Conference of the Birds,* trans. C.S. Nott (New York: Samuel Weiser, 1969), quoting from pp. 31 and 131. For a more complete verse translation see a book by the same name, trans. A. Darbandi and D. Davis (New York: Penguin Books, 1984). For a brief analysis of the work, see James W. Morris, "Reading *The Conference of the Birds,*" in W. deBary, ed., *Approaches to Asian Classics* (New York: Columbia University Press, 1990), pp. 77–85.

7. *The Wisdom of the Throne,* James W. Morris, trans. (Princeton: Princeton Library of Asian Translations, 1981), p. 256.

8. Cf. W. Montgomery Watt, "The Significance of the Early Stages of Imami Shi'ism," in N. Keddie, ed., *Religion and Politics in Iran: Shi'ism from Quietism to Revolution* (New Haven: Yale University Press, 1983), pp. 21–32.

9. For greater detail on material summarized in the following several paragraphs, see the excellent work of Nikki Keddie, *Iran: Religion, Politics, and Society* (London: Frank Cass, 1980), esp. pp. 80–118 and her *Roots of Revolution: An Interpretive History of Modern Iran* (New Haven: Yale University Press, 1981), esp. pp. 1–78; also Mangol Bayat,

Mysticism and Dissent: Socioreligious Thought in Qajar Iran (Syracuse: Syracuse University Press, 1982), esp. pp. 1–37, and "Islam in Pahlavi and Post-Pahlavi Iran: A Cultural Revolution?" in J. Esposito, ed., *Islam and Development* (Syracuse: Syracuse University Press, 1980), pp. 87–106.

10. Keddie, *Iran: Religion, Politics, and Society,* p. 97.
11. Here I am borrowing terminology from John Voll's *Islam: Continuity and Change in the Modern World* (Boulder: Westview Press, 1982), pp. 29–31.
12. Fazlur Rahman, *Islam* (Garden City: Doubleday Anchor Books, 1968), pp. 274–75.

Chapter 4

1. See A. Seguy, *The Miraculous Journey of Mahomet* (New York: Braziller, 1977); J.R. Porter, "Muhammad's Journey to Heaven," in *The Journey to the Other World,* H.R. Ellis-Davidson, ed. (Cambridge: D.S. Brewer Ltd., 1975), pp. 1–26 for the broad religio-historical background; Earle H. Waugh, "Religious Aspects of the Mi'raj Legends," *ibid.* For a primary source account, see Arthur Jeffrey, *Reader on Islam* (The Hague: Mouton, 1972), pp. 621ff.
2. *Rumi: Poet and Mystic,* R.A. Nicholson, trans. (London: Allen and Unwin, 1970), pp. 74, 87, 103, 186; see also Maneri, *The Hundred Letters,* pp. 67ff on ascent through seven levels of earthly qualities.
3. *Muslim Saints and Mystics,* A.J. Arberry, trans. (London: Routledge and Kegan Paul, 1966, and Persian Heritage Series paperback, 1979), p. 110; see also Annemarie Schimmel, *Mystical Dimensions of Islam,* p. 219.
4. Hujwiri, *Kashf al-Mahjub,* trans. R.A. Nicholson (London: Gibb Series, 1959 reprint), p. 238.

5. See e.g. J. Royster, "Muhammad as Teacher and Exemplar," *The Muslim World* 58:4 (October 1978), pp. 235–38.

6. A. Schimmel, *Mystical Dimensions of Islam,* p. 190.

7. Paul Nwyia, S.J., *Ibn Abbad de Ronda* (Beirut: Imprimerie Catholique, 1956), pp. 98–99, 232. See also *Ibn 'Abbad of Ronda: Letters on the Sufi Path,* Letter Sixteen for one spiritual director's view of the practical implications of this distinction.

8. Quoted in *The Hundred Letters,* p. 403.

9. Marshal Hodgson, *The Venture of Islam* (Chicago: University of Chicago, 1975), Vol. 1, p. 396.

10. For more on the topic see Paul Jackson, S.J., "Spiritual Guidance in the Islamic Tradition I," and J. Renard, "Spiritual Guidance in the Islamic Tradition II," in Lavinia Byrne, ed., *Traditions of Spiritual Guidance* (London: Geoffrey Chapman, 1990), pp. 188–210.

11. S.H. Nasr, "The Spiritual States in Sufism," in his *Sufi Essays* (Albany: SUNY, 1972), pp. 68–83; see esp. pp. 77ff; here quoting in modified form from p. 82.

12. *Mystical Dimensions,* p. 224.

13. *The Hundred Letters,* p. 402.

14. See H. Ritter's *Das Meer der Seele* (Leiden: Brill, 1955), pp. 18–30, for a complete summary of Attar's *Musibatname (Book of Affliction)* as well as of the poet's other major works.

15. *The Hundred Letters,* p. 402.

16. Translation from Arabic text in A.H. Farid, *Prayers of Muhammad* (Lahore: Sh. M. Ashraf, 1974), p. 217.

17. From *The Beginning of Guidance,* trans. W.M. Watt, in *The Faith and Practice of Al-Ghazali* (London: Allen and Unwin, 1970), p. 116.

18. Translated from Rumi's *Masnavi-yi Ma'navi* II:2771–79.

19. See J. Renard, "Images of Abraham in the Writings of Jalal-ad Din Rumi," *Journal of the American Oriental Society* 106:4 (1986), pp. 633–40.

20. Trans. A.J. Arberry, in *Sufism, An Account of the Mystics of Islam* (New York: Scribner's, 1970), pp. 52–53.

21. Translated from Hallaj's *Diwan*.

22. For more excellent examples of prayer, see Kenneth Cragg, *Alive to God: Muslim and Christian Prayers* (London: Allen and Unwin, 1970).

23. Further on these themes, see Fazlur Rahman, *Major Themes of the Qur'an* (Minneapolis and Chicago: Bibliotheca Islamica, 1980).

24. For more on the subject, see Thomas O'Shaughnessy, S.J., *Muhammad's Thoughts on Death: A Thematic Study of the Qur'anic Data* (Leiden: Brill, 1969), and Alford T. Welch, "Death and Dying in the Qur'an," in *Religious Encounters with Death,* Frank E. Reynolds and Earle H. Waugh, eds. (University Park: The Pennsylvania State University Press, 1977), pp. 183–89.

25. William Graham, *Divine Word and Prophetic Word in Early Islam* (The Hague: Mouton and Co., 1977), p. 202.

26. For references to Hadith on this and other subjects, see A.J. Wensinck, *A Handbook of Early Muhammadan Tradition* (Leiden: Brill, 1960), passim.

27. See A.J. Wensinck, *The Muslim Creed* (New York: Barnes and Noble, 1965), pp. 117ff, 163ff, 221ff, and Jane I. Smith, "The Understanding of *Nafs* and *Ruh* in Contemporary Muslim Considerations of the Nature of Sleep and Death," in *The Muslim World,* 69:3 (July 1979), pp. 151–62.

28. Constance Padwick, *Muslim Devotions* (London: S.P.C.K., 1961), pp. 34–35.

29. *Ibid.,* p. 277; also on mourning and popular practices, see

Kenneth Cragg, *The Dome and the Rock* (London: S.P.C.K., 1964), Chapter 19: "Death and the Muslim," pp. 205–14.

30. Padwick, *op. cit.,* p. 278.

31. Victor Turner notes that Christian pilgrims to Jerusalem, Compostela, etc., have held similar beliefs; see his "Death and the Dead in the Pilgrimage Process," in *Religious Encounters with Death,* pp. 24–39.

32. Translated from Arabic text in A.H. Farid, *Prayers of Muhammad* (Lahore: Sh. Muhammad Ashraf, 1974), p. 185. Further details on funeral practices relating to customs surviving from pre-Islamic times in I. Goldziher, "On the Veneration of the Dead in Paganism and Islam," in his *Muslim Studies* (London: Allen and Unwin, 1967), Vol. I, pp. 209–38.

33. Padwick, *op. cit.,* pp. 280–81.

34. Earle Waugh, "Muharram Rites: Community Death and Rebirth," in *Religious Encounters with Death,* p. 205. For more on the passion play see G. von Gruenebaum, *Muhammadan Festivals* (London: Curzon Press, 1976), pp. 85–94; Mahmoud Ayoub, *Redemptive Suffering in Islam* (The Hague: Mouton and Co., 1978) and "The Problem of Suffering in Islam," in *Journal of Dharma* (July 1977), pp. 267–94.

35. A.J. Arberry, trans., *Mystical Poems of Rumi* (Chicago: University of Chicago Press, 1968), pp. 122–23.

36. *The Hundred Letters,* pp. 407–11.

37. *The Conference of the Birds,* C.S. Nott, trans. (New York: Samuel Weiser, 1954), pp. 106–07.

38. *The Hundred Letters,* p. 146.

39. William Graham, *Divine Word and Prophetic Word in Early Islam* (The Hague: Mouton, 1977), pp. 182–83.

40. Translated from Rumi's *Diwan-i Shams* 2048:6–8.

41. A. Schimmel, *The Triumphal Sun* (London: Fine Books, 1978), pp. 278–79.
42. Margaret Smith, *Readings from the Mystics of Islam* (London: Allen and Unwin, 1972), p. 27.
43. "The Four Quartets."

Epilogue

1. For further detail on the American Muslim scene, see especially Yvonne Haddad, *Islamic Values in the United States* (New York: Oxford University Press, 1987) and her excellent brief survey, "A Century of Islam in America," *The Muslim World Today,* Occasional Paper No. 4 (Washington, D.C.: Islamic Affairs Programs, 1986).
2. For more on Muslims' perceptions of their cultural and social experience of life in America, see Elias Mallon, *Neighbors: Muslims in North America* (Louisville: Presbyterian Publishing House, 1990), and Allen Richardson, *Islamic Cultures in North America: Patterns of Belief and Devotion of Muslims from Asian Countries in the United States and Canada* (New York: Pilgrim Press, 1981).

Index

Aaron, 28
Abd al-Muttalib, 40
Abraham, 5, 8, 10, 48, 137, 148; and
 the Ka'ba, 6; in the Qur'an, 28,
 39, 54–55; as prophet, 44, 51,
 147; and interreligious relations,
 80–81; journey to Makka, 83
Abu Bakr, 52, 53, 88, 98, 145
Abu Hanifa, 108
Abu Sa'id al-Khudri, 48
Abu Talib, 40
Adam, 27, 28, 43, 45, 62, 63, 83,
 133, 140
Adaptationist, 115, 117, 120
Afghanistan, 24, 78, 111
Africa, 106, 156
African-Americans, 156–158
Agha Khan, 99
Ahmad, Khurshid, 69
Akhbaris, 111
Al-Aqsa mosque, 124
Ali, 36, 40, 98, 99, 110
Ali, Noble Drew, 157
Allah, Western view of, 17; images
 of, 18, 28, 135, 141; ninety-nine
 names of, 19–20; and the
 Throne Verse, 22, 135; and the
 Verse of Light, 24; and pre-
 destination, 24, 63; and *jihad*,
 49–55, 61; and Abraham, 55,
 87; revealed in creation, 56, 63,
 128; Mu'tazilite view of, 65;

and pilgrimage, 83, 92; and
 judgment, 91; and revelation,
 102; transcendent, 118–19; and
 spirituality, 118, 126–28; and
 moral valuation, 119; and
 Muhammad, 133–34; and
 prayer, 135–40; mystic view of,
 138–139; and Qur'an, 141
America(n), view of Arab world,
 17, 75–77; relations with Iran,
 67, 101. *See also* Persian Gulf
 War; United States
Anthropomorphism, 35–36
Arabia, 40
Arafat (in Arabia), 87–88
Ascension, 5, 123–24, 151–52
Asceticism, 129, 133
Ash'ari, 35, 36
Asia, 5, 53, 106
Attar, Farid ad-Din, 92–93, 125,
 127, 133–34, 147
Aya(t), See Signs
Azrael (angel), 148

Baghdad, 101, 106, 129
Bahira, 40
Bangladesh, 156
Bani Sadr, Abulhasan, 67
Bedouin, 40
Bible, 11, 29, 62–63. *See also*
 Scripture, Christian

172

Qur'an (*continued*)
124; referred to in the Qur'an,
30, 96; Makkan Period, 31;
Madinan Period, 31, 93; on
monotheism, 31, 78; on
Judgment, 31, 91, 141; style of,
31, 34; and worship, 32–33, 91;
and Night of Power, 33, 41;
interpretation of, 34–38, 106–07;
116–17; and Mu'tazilites, 35;
and Shi'ites, 36; and Al-Ash'ari,
36; and mysticism, 37–39,
126–28; and Hadith, 43,
103–05; on Abraham, 44,
54–55; on Moses, 44; on Hijra,
53; on creation, 56; on money,
58–59, 64, 69, 140; on jihad,
60–62; on the environment,
62–64; relations with other religions, 78–81; on community,
94; on leadership, 97; and
Truth, 117–18; on sin, 139;
on death, 140–41, 144, 149
Quraysh, 40, 41, 43, 52, 61, 86

Rabi'a, 129
Rahman, Fazlur, 116, 139
Rajab (month of), 41
Ramadan, 33, 41, 57
Rasul, See Messengers
Rationalists, 38. *See also* Mu'tazilites
Ra'y, 105
Reason, 65, 115, 118, 120
Religio-cultural styles, 116–17
Religious orders, 129–30
Revelation, 12, 28, 32, 34, 39, 63,
102, 106, 115. *See also* Qur'an
Revivalist, 116
Riba, 69
Roman Catholic, 15, 105

Rumi, Jalal ad-Din, 52, 53, 89, 90,
124, 136, 137, 147, 150, 151
Rushdie, Salman, 75
Russia, 67, 78

Sacred space, 58–60
Sadiq, Ja'far al-, 99
Sadra, Mulla, 93
Safa, 87, 88
Safavid Dynasty, 108, 109, 111
Saj', 31
Salat, 56, 94, 135–37, 155
Salih, 43
Sana'i of Ghazna, 23
Satan, 137
Saudi Arabia, 17, 74, 77, 86
Scripture, Islamic, 1, 9, 13, 23, 29,
30, 33, 34, 35, 38, 44. *See also*
Qur'an; Christian, 28, 30, 33;
Jewish, 19, 28, 39, 81, 85
Sensus fidelium, 105
Seveners, *See* Isma'ilis
Sha'ban, 146
Shafi'i, Idris al-, 106, 115
Shari'a, 10, 12, 47, 74, 83, 127
Shaykh, 53, 89, 90, 129
Shaykhulislam, 110
Sheba, Queen of, 92
Shi'i, 10; on interpretation of
Qur'an, 36; and Ali, 36, 98;
and succession, 98–99; on
economics, 64, 66, 68; and
eschatology, 100; and Iran,
101; and law schools, 108–109,
111; and Safavid Dynasty, 109;
and Pahlavi Dynasty, 113; and
spirituality, 118; and death,
146. *See also* Seveners;
Twelvers
Shirk, 61, 66

Of Related Interest

Responses to 101 Questions on Islam
John Renard
Paperback   3803-4   192 pages $12.95

In the learner-friendly style of the *101 Questions* series, John Renard's study of Islam for Christians gives a practical overview of the beliefs and customs of Islam in today's world. Renard discusses:

- ❖ Sources
- ❖ History
- ❖ Beliefs and Doctrines
- ❖ Law and Ethics
- ❖ Spirituality and Mysticism
- ❖ Cultural and Intellectual Contributions
- ❖ Relationship to Christianity
- ❖ Women and Family
- ❖ Global and Geopolitical Issues